"This book performs an important service to the field of risk management by bringing together research spanning the various disciplines that have taken an interest in the field. In doing so, it advances our understanding of enterprise risk management and clarifies the concept of strategic risk management. The book provides an important base on which future development of research in strategic risk management will rest."

— *Philip Bromiley, Dean's Professor in Strategic Management,*
Merage School of Business, University of California, Irvine

T0384090

Strategic Risk Management

Organizations face challenges in adapting their current business and operational activities to dynamic contexts. Successful companies share a common characteristic of dealing with the emergent risks and threats in responses that generate viable solutions.

Strategic risk management (SRM) is a multidisciplinary and rather fractured field of study, which creates significant challenges for research. This short-form book constitutes an expert overview of the topic, providing insight into the theory and practice.

Essential reading for strategic management researchers, the authors frame the fundamental principles, emerging challenges and responses for the future, which will also provide valuable insights for adjacent business disciplines and beyond.

Torben Juul Andersen is a Professor of Strategy and International Management and Director of the Global Strategic Responsiveness Initiative at the Copenhagen Business School.

Johanna Sax received her PhD in Strategic Risk Management from the Copenhagen Business School where she is engaged as a Censor and is a Research Associate with the Department of International Economics, Government and Business.

State of the Art in Business Research
Edited by Professor Geoffrey Wood

Recent advances in theory, methods, and applied knowledge (alongside structural changes in the global economic ecosystem) have presented researchers with challenges in seeking to stay abreast of their fields and navigate new scholarly terrains.

State of the Art in Business Research presents short-form books that provide an expert map to guide readers through new and rapidly evolving areas of research. Each title will provide an overview of the area, a guide to the key literature and theories, and time-saving summaries of how theory interacts with practice.

As a collection, these books provide a library of theoretical and conceptual insights, and exposure to novel research tools and applied knowledge, that aid and facilitate in defining the state of the art, as a foundation stone for a new generation of research.

Flexible Working in Organizations
A Research Overview
Clare Kelliher and Lilian M. de Menezes

Network Industries
A Research Overview
Matthias Finger

Strategic Risk Management
A Research Overview
Torben Juul Andersen and Johanna Sax

For more information about this series, please visit: www.routledge.com/State-of-the-Art-in-Business-Research/book-series/START

Strategic Risk Management
A Research Overview

**Torben Juul Andersen and
Johanna Sax**

Routledge
Taylor & Francis Group

LONDON AND NEW YORK

First published 2020
by Routledge
4 Park Square, Milton Park, Abingdon, Oxon OX14 4RN

and by Routledge
605 Third Avenue, New York, NY 10017

First issued in paperback 2022

Routledge is an imprint of the Taylor & Francis Group, an informa business

© 2020 Torben Juul Andersen and Johanna Sax

Publisher's Note
The publisher has gone to great lengths to ensure the quality of this reprint but points out that some imperfections in the original copies may be apparent.

British Library Cataloguing-in-Publication Data
A catalogue record for this book is available from the British Library

Library of Congress Cataloging-in-Publication Data
A catalog record has been requested for this book

ISBN 13: 978-1-03-247536-3 (pbk)
ISBN 13: 978-1-138-31534-1 (hbk)
ISBN 13: 978-0-429-45638-1 (ebk)

DOI: 10.4324/9780429456381

Typeset in Times New Roman
by codeMantra

Contents

1 Introduction

Contemporary organizations whether private or public are faced with the daunting task of navigating through increasingly turbulent conditions adapting their current business and operational activities to often rapidly changing contexts (Slywotzky and Drzik, 2005). The underlying strategic issues are becoming more problematic, harder to identify, more anxiety-provoking, and hence difficult to manage (Beck, 1992; Gephart, Van Maanen and Oberlechner, 2009). In many instances, we observe dysfunctional behaviors that can hinder effective responses to the emergent risks as decision-makers cling to the status quo in attempts to weather the storm (Samuelson and Zeckhauser, 1988) or bury their heads in the sand to avoid the discomforting feelings around the impending risks (Shimizu and Hitt, 2004). The ability to adapt the organization and its strategy to the changing business environment is a central issue in the management field, and it is challenged by a changing risk landscape (Andersen, 2015). The extended global reach of organizations facilitated by digital technologies increase the level of uncertainty in the business environment that can be conceived as a dynamic complex system. Many interacting entities (and agents in them) where each component affects the others can lead to nonlinear outcomes that defeat a simple aggregation of actions and make eventual effects hard to foresee. Add to this the observed occurrence of extreme events ascribing a role to randomness that contravenes common statistical approaches to probability (Taleb, 2007a). Nonetheless, the most successful companies seem to share a common characteristic of being able to actually confront those strategic issues and deal with the emergent risks and threats in responses that generate viable solutions. We might argue that these organizations are effective at executing strategic risk management (SRM).

Parts of the strategy, management accounting, and corporate finance literatures suggest that firms should engage in proactive practices of strategic risk-taking as the means to overcome the inherent uncertainties associated with major decisions (Priem, Rasheed and Kotulic, 1995; Simons, 1995a, 1995b; Damodaran, 2007; Andersen, Garvey and Roggi, 2014). Hence, strategic risk-taking – trying out new responsive initiatives – has become a vital element of business conduct and an essential source of competitive advantage (Chatterjee et al., 2003). Nevertheless, capitalizing effectively on risk-taking requires a high level of strategic response capabilities (Bettis and Hitt, 1995), adaptive capabilities (Volberda, 1996), and dynamic capabilities (Teece, Pisano and Shuen, 1997). These conditions are studied in the field of strategic management but obviously relate to a much broader set of academic disciplines. Hence, the study of SRM – as strategic management itself – is multidisciplinary in nature and integrates a diversity of perspectives and analytical techniques originating from different academic fields. In view of this, several scholars and practitioners have called for the inclusion of diverse functional perspectives, considering the link between risk management and strategic planning as essentially representing comparable processes to be integrated (Chatterjee et al., 2003; Bromiley et al., 2014).

Risk management processes such as enterprise risk management (ERM), the core content of which can trace its characteristic elements to inputs from different academic fields, attempts to portray an active approach to deal with the (major) risks of contemporary organizations. The ERM approach has received increasing attention among practitioners and academics alike to become a predominant prescriptive risk management approach. Initially, risk management evolved from insurance and financial management to become a managerial discipline grounded in the control aspects of operations management, management accounting and auditing. Over the years, the risk management discourse has intensified to become an essential source of governance and general management principles (Power, 2007). Hence, it is argued that "risk and risk management have come to play a key role in the very idea of organizing and organization itself" (Scheytt et al., 2006, p. 1336).

The *Routledge Companion to Strategic Risk Management* (2016) was a sign of the mounting interest and relevance of the so-called 'strategic' exposures in all types of organizations as an inevitable consequence of the turbulent environments they operate in. The *Companion* revealed the multidisciplinary nature ascribed to SRM – a relatively poorly defined concept with different meanings to different people depending on their background, professional anchoring, managerial perspective, and purpose of focusing on something referred to as strategic risks.

Hence, the *Companion* was purposely organized as a diverse exposé of different contributions including (obviously) some strategic management views, but also incorporating economic, financial, psychological, cognitive, and ethical leadership perspectives with contributions from academia as well as engaged practitioners caring for the topic. This opens the issue as to whether prevailing risk management practice is leading academia, or whether scientific research influences practical applications of risk management. While the former can be claimed with some conviction in the case of risk management, it is probably safe to say (at least) that different academic fields interact with risk management praxis where we can see mutual influences and spill-over effects in either direction. As a consequence, we may argue for a certain convergence between academic and practice views on risk management, although with some divergent perspectives that serve to critique and (hopefully) improve current practices.

Strategic risks, and as a consequence SRM, are not unilaterally defined terms or concepts. To the contrary, strategic risks are generally understood and depicted (if they are explicitly defined) in quite different ways across various academic fields as well as by different professional communities (Bromiley, Rau and McShane, 2016). A financial risk perspective may, for example, refer to price volatility that can affect the value of the firm, uncertainty that can affect firm performance, external events that can affect shareholder value. A risk perspective adopted by regulators may emphasize, say, events that affect an organization's strategy, failure to adopt the right strategy or executing the chosen strategy properly, potential shortfalls in earnings and capital caused by changes in the business environment. Financial management could refer risk to, for example, high levels of resource commitments, substantial commitments made to gain superior returns, and significant business investments with uncertain outcomes. A planning perspective may subscribe risk to, for example, the most consequential (internal and external) influences on the ability to execute the strategy, unexpected changes in strategy formulation, events that affect the strategic objectives, and factors that influence the ability to achieve objectives. A contingency view may refer to the implications of, for example, competitor, technology, and political risk factors and changes in economic, political, and competitive conditions. Consider on top of this that the term 'strategic' added to anything may simply serve to make it appear more significant or important. That could partially explain what is happening, but a general trait across all the noted references is, that the potential impact or ultimate effects are deemed to be substantial and in the extreme represent life-threatening concerns. Yet, the various definitions assume, or imply, slight variation in the range of factors considered, say, from financial price volatility to changes in economic conditions – and/or the way strategic management is conceived, ranging from top-down planning to bottom-up emergent strategy.

Due to the cross-disciplinary origins of risk management and the evolution to eventually become ERM, it has assumed and incorporated (many) different functional perspectives that clearly influence the perception of the type of risk factors that appear on the radar screen of those involved in the process. As the field of strategy itself is not a clearly defined academic discipline, or field of study, but entertains many different views and perspectives. The concept of SRM is no different in this regard. Strategy can adopt different theoretical rationales, say, from industrial economics to resource-based logics, different perspectives from content to a process view, and different dynamics from causal to effectual. Similar distinctions can be traced to different depictions of SRM as process frameworks, techniques, and analytical tools, employing different practice rationales. In view of this backdrop, it is quite understandable why we observe multiple definitions and views on the concept of SRM. Maybe it is even alright to accept that status, as long as we understand the reasons for its existence and underpinnings, and use it as a way to (potentially) triangulate a diversity of insights to better understand a notoriously complex field that has received increasing attention from various interest groups over recent years.

The organizational application of risk management practices, arguably a precursor to SRM, grew out of an early insurance focus with a prime objective of arranging economic covers for possible adverse high-impact risk events, including different casualties and hazards. This is the basis for risk diversification through organized insurance markets as efficient mechanisms to resolve those problems. The insurance departments, many of which still exist in contemporary organizations, gradually extended their focus to also consider more general risk management concerns. The gradual liberalization of international transactions and abolishment of fixed-rate regimes increased the volatility of foreign exchange markets and spurred a professional focus on financial risk management. The advancement toward more sophisticated models to value options, derivative instrument, and aggregated portfolio exposures, including concepts like value-at-risk and the like, promoted particularly quantitative and calculative risk management approaches. The portfolio perspective gave partial impetus to the idea that the intricate relationships between various risk factors should be taken into consideration when determining the aggregated organizational exposures. It coincided with the idea that risk management should adopt an integrated view across all types of risk across the entire enterprise as a better way to manage corporate exposures. The mantra of the risk management departments became a focus on enterprise-wide risk management practices, where individual silos of specialized risk management functions were supposed to become parts of an integrated risk management function. A modern portfolio theoretical perspective implies that less than completely correlated financial rates, or risk factors in general, will diversify away some of the aggregated exposure. However, the 2008 financial crisis demonstrated that international financial markets constitute a dynamic complex system where unexpected things can happen as financial rates exacerbate each other and thereby increase the aggregated exposures across the entire system of market participants.

There was an increased focus on multinational financial management theory considering the effects of foreign exchange and interest rate exposures in complex multinational organizations, including the potential effects on (sizeable) cross-border investments entailing highly uncertain political and sovereign risks that can be very difficult to discern and insure. Various perspectives in the field of operations management, including new approaches such as total quality control and lean processes, added to the repertoire that could be ascribed to the risk management function. While these perspectives are primarily linked to the internal operations of the organization, they still provide some very important and relevant aspects of the total risk management concept. The operational concerns have more recently been extended to consider the vulnerability of international value-chains to disruptions caused by various physical, economic, and political phenomena. In the context of the larger global economy, these types of events are well beyond the control of corporate management and are highly unpredictable, thereby adding new strategic dimensions to the enterprise-wide risk management challenge.

A number of large corporate scandals in the early 2000s, including, for example, Enron, WorldCom, and Tyco Int'l, induced major political initiatives, such as, the influential Sarbanes-Oxley Act in the USA in 2002. This legislation imposed (more) direct personal responsibility on top executives, and members of the board, to provide accurate financial reporting and impose proper corporate risk practices. This further spurred a movement toward ERM as a formal set of practices aimed to guarantee that appropriate risk management processes were in place, and not least, that executives could demonstrate that they had been implemented. The emergence of ERM frameworks was to a large extent inspired by professional interests with a focus on internal control processes practiced in management accounting and related ex post monitoring approaches in the auditing profession (COSO, 2004). The financial crisis and the devastating effect on some otherwise well-established financial institutions spurred a subsequent process for more vigorous pursuit of formal ERM practices now increasingly dominated by two major (competing) standards: COSO and ISO 31000 (COSO, 2004; ISO, 2009).

The immediate aftermath of the financial crisis in 2008 led to much soul searching including a realization that moral standards and ethical conduct exerted a lot of influence on the course of events before and up to the financial market collapse (RiskMinds, 2009). As things have evolved since then, policy-makers and regulators, particularly in the financial sector, have enforced more rigorous reporting of risk imposing formal ERM procedures on financial intermediaries. This development has also formalized the requirement for the so-called high-level chief risk officers (CROs) in banks as a way to establish independent risk management functions with resources and direct access to the governance level (BIS, 2015).

The experiences from increasingly globalized business activities during the decades before the turn of the millennium increased exposures to the so-called strategic risks in the form of potentially high-impact competitive, economic, and (sovereign) political factors, the effects of which were eloquently depicted by Slywotzky and Drzik (2005) as the largest and most important of all risks. In the financial industry, the extended risk perspective was primarily devoted to an increased emphasis on operational risks, which is understandable given the extreme number of physical clearing and bookkeeping transactions carried out in this industry every day. It was initially aimed at applications of advanced quantitative methodologies to determine these exposures in individual organizations, but has later been relaxed (after the financial crisis) realizing that these exposures are indeed very difficult to quantify (BIS, 2015).

Strategic risks in the financial industry, for example, considering the effects of competition from new more efficient intermediation technologies, have only rarely been considered by the regulators although with some notable exceptions (e.g., Carse, 1999; Kroszner, 2008). When these risks are considered in the academic literature, it typically considers the potential effects on lost earnings related to an institutional capital buffer required to withstand potential systemic effects (e.g., Chockalingam, Dabadhgao and Soetekouw, 2018). Hence, no methodologies have been developed to consider how these types of risk can be addressed and mitigated in the first place. Instead, there seems to be an increased emphasis on application of formal ERM frameworks on financial institutions as the way to safeguard better risk practices (e.g., Arndorfer and Minto, 2015). The same tendency is observed in Europe as the proper way to guide risk management practices in large firms required to report on major exposures and internal risk management practices (FERMA/ECIIA, 2014).

These ERM frameworks all contain the same kernel of identifying, assessing, mitigating, and monitoring various risks possibly identified in the form of ascertaining and searching across different classifications of risk, say, hazards, financial/economic, operational, and strategic risk categories. However, as you move toward nonfinancial risks such as the operational and strategic types of risk, the general experience is that it becomes increasingly difficult to foresee specific risk events and harder to quantify potential effects. So, there is a dilemma associated with the application of formal risk management frameworks to deal with the largest risks, assuming that they can be identified and handled in advance. Under all circumstances, it is pretty clear to discern from this evolutionary development that the fields referred to as enterprise risk management (ERM) and strategic risk management (SRM) are influenced by a multitude of academic and professional disciplines as well as associated political and institutional interests.

All the while, it may also explain why it can be hard to clearly distinguish between ERM and SRM, where the proponents of the former tend to argue that ERM also considers strategic risks (e.g., Frigo and Anderson, 2001) whereas proponents of the latter argue that ERM is still quite immature in its ability to manage strategic risks (e.g., Andersen and Schrøder, 2010). Hence, both ERM and SRM derived from within an evolving field of enterprise-wide risk management concerns and a variety of (inter-)related professional (sub-)fields. As the formal ERM frameworks have evolved, they now constitute a well-established set of institutionalized interests and practices, whereas the same cannot be said about SRM. Rather, SRM is arguably positioned as being somewhat critical to hardcore believers in the sufficiency of ERM to deal effectively with all the major risks of the organization. The argument is that while ERM, in its essence, builds on an ability to identify, foresee, and prepare, there is less capacity, or capabilities, to deal with true uncertainty and the unpredictable context that characterize specifically the operational and strategic types of risks.

Furthermore, developments are influenced by various entities with special concerns, including policy-makers and regulatory bodies, interest groups, and professional institutions with capital and resources committed to pursue particular views on both SRM and ERM. All the while, there are few unifying academic journals, or research communities, that maintain a distinct focus on SRM issues. The topic of SRM is often dismissed as only peripherally related to the issues discussed among conventional strategy scholars while it equally fails to comply with the ways adopted in established fields such as management accounting and auditing. This obviously represents a challenge to the extent that SRM may deserve further scrutiny and development as a (potentially) important way to deal with the organizational, managerial, governance, and leadership challenges of our time that urgently need (it seems) better and more effective responses.

This evolutionary account frames this research overview of the SRM field and provides the backdrop for the remaining chapters. So, we are faced with a rather fragmented evolving field of study with strong roots and relationships to the ideas about an overarching (enterprise) risk management approach with risk governance practices to support organization-level strategic outcomes that deal effectively with the changing risk landscape. The status of current state-of-the-art risk management approaches have a number of common denominators founded on the predominance of two major control-based frameworks that are emerging as the global standards for the ERM practices. However, we also recognize (and the frameworks do themselves to some extent as well) that the effects of the prescribed practices are (or can be heavily) influenced by human bias and behavior, where (core) values and ethics play essential roles. Human psychology and cognitive biases often influence the players at the highest governance and policy-making levels, illustrating that we need more than standard practices for individuals and systems within the organization. All the while, contemporary organizations are exposed to environmental threats with large existential consequences caused by (potentially) extreme events that go beyond resolutions by individual organizations, but require new collaborative solutions that engage broader social networks. This points to the significance of dealing more squarely on these types of strategic risks, that not only can make or break prevailing firm-specific advantages, but may change the economic viability and long-term sustainability of business and society as we know it today. There seems to be an urgent need to consider how we can develop effective 'strategic' risk management capabilities to deal with this emerging environmental context.

In conclusion, one of the underlying challenges of the (strategic) risk management field is the multidisciplinary nature of the topic, which has evolved from rather distinct, but far from coordinated perspectives and approaches with limited mutual awareness. This has led to fragmented views of the field with different conceptualizations, purposes, and definitions of risk, thus resulting in different approaches and normative practices. While the diversity of perspective constitutes a potential strength of the field that opens for triangulated studies of the phenomenon that can gain from cross-fertilization between various subfields and create new valuable insights, this potential still has to come to (full) fruition. In the meanwhile, common practices and standards are leading the way further enforced by public policy-making, although the empirical evidence to support these approaches continues to be in short supply. In the ensuing chapters, we will provide an overview of relevant research contributions to SRM for an updated status of the field with views on possible directions for future studies.

Chapter 2 provides a general background for the concept of SRM, presenting different definitions and perspectives to illustrate the origins and inspirational sources of the field and its current manifestations for practice. We particularly link to research streams in strategic management and financial economics for underlying value-creating rationales partially embedded in a theoretical conundrum between the ability to form unique value-creating risk management capabilities in contrast to implementing broadly promoted advantages from formal ERM practices. Risk has always been a central concern in management studies as well as other fields of study with different perspectives on the risk management challenge including the emergence of ERM frameworks that claim to deal with total exposures including operational and strategic risks.

Chapter 3 presents some foundational studies with concepts and frameworks that form the basis for the risk concept, its relationship to strategic issues, and various ways proposed to manage strategic risk, including implementation of ERM frameworks. Strategy scholars have conceptualized risk for decades, considering the ability to manage inherent exposures in strategic decision processes through strategic issue management systems. The contemporary ERM approaches establish ex ante risk assessment and ex post diagnostic controls to help ensure fulfillment of objectives implicitly, assuming strategy setting by top management and the board based on development of guiding risk appetite statements for the organization. It is also argued that ERM can be applied interactively with ongoing strategy-making in ways that integrate the risk management processes with ongoing strategic decision processes.

Chapter 4 outlines various empirical studies that represent the current evidence and insights to inform the field of SRM derived from past and current research efforts, including antecedents for ERM, ERM performance effects, and contingencies for successful ERM adoption. While the empirical literature remains relatively scarce, there has been an increasing focus on the conditions around the adoption of ERM practices, the proposed benefits, and the ability to deal with major strategic exposures. The results from the various empirical studies are less than conclusive, although there is emerging evidence that adherence to the basic principles of ERM can be integrated with strategic planning to generate value. Nonetheless, further research is required to uncover the finer nuances associated with SRM and its possible effects where future management studies can uncover important behavioral, cognitive, and ethical influences on organizational risk management capabilities.

Chapter 5 summarizes what we see as some emerging themes in studies of SRM, including the effects of organizational structure, cognitive biases, and psychological factors in human systems as important areas for future research. It considers the challenge of dealing effectively with true uncertainty that is hard to quantify and foresee (as opposed to risk as measurable uncertainty) and the potential for extreme events in increasingly dynamic and complex environments. This may build on and extend insights inspired by research on high-reliability organizations, operational resilience, stakeholder relationships, responsible behaviors, ethical issues, corporate values, and organizational culture.

2 Background, concepts, and frameworks

One of the first considerations of risk in the context of strategic management appeared in an article by Fiegenbaum and Thomas (1986) in the *Strategic Management Journal* where they urged more focus on risk and its implications for strategic managers. The risk concept (has) had different meanings (and measures) in different academic fields, where finance typically refers to the distribution of market returns as opposed to managerial judgment and (firm-level) consequences of (strategic) decisions in management. Bettis (1983) specifically pinpointed the conundrum that modern finance theory assumes no rewards to unsystematic firm-specific risk whereas "it lies at the heart of strategic management" (Bettis, 1983, p. 406). By applying variance-based firm-level performance measures of risk, Bowman (1984) promoted a 'total risk' concept as being of relevance for corporate managers. This implies handling a portfolio that incorporates all types of risk across the entire organization and managing their aggregated effects on firm-level (strategic) outcomes. Although market- and accounting-based return measures normally co-vary, Bowman (1980) found an inverse relationship between average (accounting) returns and the standard deviation of returns, which is in contrast to the positive correlations between systematic risk and market returns considered in finance theory. This so-called risk/return paradox in strategic management – often referred to as the Bowman paradox – has subsequently been subject to intense scrutiny in the strategy field (e.g., Nickel and Rodriguez, 2002; Andersen, Denrell and Bettis, 2007; Henkel, 2009). These variance-based measures of total risk have been used regularly by management scholars in different organizational studies, although it by no means constitutes the only, or the primary, approach to risk research in the strategy field.

The business environment and industry dynamic is an important aspect of strategy (e.g., Porter, 1979), as is managerial judgment (e.g., Vlek and Stallen, 1980), the organizational context, and the way the situation is presented or framed (e.g., Tversky and Kahneman, 1981). The risk propensity of strategic decision-makers determines risk-taking and strategic outcomes and is in turn influenced by a multitude of factors in the external business environment and industry context as well as by internal organizational and individual characteristics (Baird and Thomas, 1985). This contingency approach has inspired a broad research stream on managerial risk-taking in the strategy field over the years assuming different theoretical perspectives (e.g., Hoskisson et al., 2017). A common approach has considered the implications of conflicts between (typically top-level) executives and firm shareholders adopting an agency theoretical perspective that promotes alignment between ownership and managerial incentives (e.g., Jensen and Meckling, 1976). A sizeable research literature has analyzed strategic risk-taking from a behavioral perspective where executives (are assumed to) base their decisions on current firm performance compared to different predetermined aspiration levels (e.g., Cyert and March, 1963). Another important strand of research has evolved from upper echelons theory where the risk perceptions of executive decision-makers are affected by personal characteristics as they construe a reality that inform major strategic decisions (e.g., Hambrick, 2007). This research has investigated potential effects of psychological executive properties, including effects caused by self-evaluation, overconfidence, narcissism, hybris, and humbleness. The backgrounds, experiences, and diversity of chief executive officers (CEOs) as well as the social and behavioral integration of the top management teams (TMTs) may also exert an influence on the way important decisions are made and operational initiatives executed across the organization. These factors are seen as possible antecedents for adverse outcomes caused by excessive risk-taking, possibly linked to unethical behavior, or extreme risk aversion to the detriment of innovation and generation of opportunities.

A risk contingency view

The contingency perspective to strategic risk-taking (Baird and Thomas, 1985) implies that it is possible to identify important antecedent factors that with some likelihood will induce particular organizational behaviors and/or strategic decision outcomes. In other words, it reflects the idea of proactively identifying influential factors in advance – on an ex ante basis – as a way to discern potential subsequent adverse, or beneficial, effects or outcomes. This perspective can be used to identify particular risk contingencies in advance as a way to consider possible consequences and manage outcomes proactively to enhance opportunities and/or prepare to deal with adverse developments. Risk is visible in other management fields as well. In the international business field, Mascarenhas (1982) observed periods of discontinuous change and environmental instability that create disparities in economic growth, energy and resource supplies, foreign exchange rates, and political and government actions that, coupled with unfamiliarity with diverse cultures and societies, challenge international firms. Similarly, Ghoshal (1987, p. 429) observes that "a multinational corporation faces many different kinds of risks, some of which are endemic to all firms and some others are unique to organizations operating across national boundaries." He refers to different types of macroeconomic, policy, competitive, and resource risks that can affect the performance of a multinational enterprise (Ghoshal, 1987). Ghoshal (1987) further identifies economic efficiency, risk management, and innovation capacity as three value-creating drivers of the multinational enterprise. Efficiency derives from optimizing the geographical location of the organization structure, where risk management considers the flexibility, or optionality, needed to fend off the effects from unexpected changes, and innovation is the creative potential to be derived from a changing global context.

Miller (1992) considered an analytical framework to identify general environmental risks, industry-related risks, and internal firm-related risks as a way to manage the multinational firm more effectively. The general environmental risks include the potential effects of macroeconomic, political, and social factors, whereas industry risks relate to changes in demand, supply, and competitive conditions. The internal firm-related risks consider managerial and behavioral deficiencies, product and market liabilities, operational and value-chain disruptions, development uncertainties, and the quality of receivables. Miller (1992) recognizes the limitations of market-based financial hedging and discusses strategic (risk) management as the means to avoid, control, and diversify exposures, or adapting through cooperation and establishing sufficient flexibilities in the operating structure of the organization. In management accounting, Simons (2000) introduces a somewhat comparable framework that first considers the overarching franchise risks and then gradually narrows the scope to consider competitive risks, asset impairment risks, operational risks, and, finally, business risks. This reflect a similar way to structure the types, or classes, of risks that may affect the organization from broad-based external influences to more internally focused factors that altogether affect the current business. In short, these approaches prevail in different management fields and are reflected in different risk classification schemes, which typically categorize different types of influencing factors, such as hazards, financial, operational, and strategic risks (e.g., Andersen and Schrøder, 2010; McShane, 2018).

So, strategic thinking frequently includes considerations about the possible effects from risk and uncertainty as potential inhibitors and adaptive opportunity-makers in the strategy-making process. In the strategy field, there is broad consensus (today) that strategy-making constitutes a mixture of top management-driven intended (or induced) strategic planning and strategic emergence from autonomous initiatives taken throughout the organization (e.g., Mintzberg and Waters, 1985; Burgelman and Grove, 1995, 2007). Conventional strategic management – as taught in most business schools – reflects a rational analytical approach to determine a strategic path formed by analyses of the external and internal environments and (typically) synthesized in an SWOT analysis (conferring strengths, weaknesses, opportunities, and threats) to identify strategic alternatives (e.g., Andrews, 1987; Ansoff, 1987; Andersen, 2000, 2004). Hence, a conventional strategic planning approach implies that strategy is formed as an analytical thought process, where the resulting plan (subsequently) is to be implemented by the organization with regular controls to monitor realized outcomes compared to the planned targets and benchmarks. It is also argued that the associated analyses of external and internal environments constitute a form of strategic risk assessment that can be linked to a formal process of managing the total portfolio of corporate risks (e.g., Andersen and Schrøder, 2010).

A corporate risk management view

Corporate risk management, also referred to as traditional risk management by some, has primarily been focused on insurable and transferable risks that can be quantified and hence exchanged or traded in professional markets. Hence, the initial corporate approaches to risk management had their roots primarily from within the insurance and finance disciplines (McShane, 2018). As conventional risk management was mostly focused on quantifiable hazards and financial risks, the consideration for 'total' risk management requires a broader focus to also consider the harder-to-quantify operational and strategic risks. As noted, much of the management literature has considered the broader spectrum of environmental risks ranging from global sociopolitical factors to the competitive dynamic of the industry with a view to the firm-specific conditions (e.g., Ghoshal, 1987; Miller, 1992; Simons, 2000). A corporate finance perspective suggests that effective firms differentiate between the identified risks and only hedge those (possibly financial) risks that may defeat specific corporate risk management skills, while exposures to strategic risks where the firm is expected to have unique risk management capabilities can be increased to gain comparative risk-taking advantages (e.g., Nocco and Stulz, 2006; Damodaran, 2007).

The strategic planning and corporate finance perspectives can be identified in much of the thinking behind the predominant enterprise risk management (ERM) perspectives that tout a holistic approach integrating all risks to avoid suboptimal behaviors in isolated silos of specialized risk functions (e.g., Culp, 2001). They often adopt a distinct governance perspective, assuming that the TMT and the board can determine and formulate a precise 'risk appetite' statement as a guide to resource committing decisions throughout the organization. Hence, in principle, this should be able to support both strategic decisions around top management and (emergent) operational decisions made throughout the organization with the intent of optimizing the risk-adjusted return of the corporation (Nocco and Stulz, 2006). This thinking obviously contravenes the traditional views implied by the application of Capital Asset Pricing Model (CAPM) thinking and modern portfolio theory, which fundamentally argues that management of firm-specific risk is superfluous since it can be diversified away by investors. So, it also implies that some of the conventional risk management rationales in finance has been revised and updated.

The way risk has been considered in corporate finance and multinational financial management is to apply risk-adjusted discount rates to evaluate future cash flows that are exposed to specific commercial and sovereign risks (e.g., Moffett, Stonehill and Eiteman, 2008; Brealey, Myers and Allen, 2011). The idea being that a risky investment must provide a higher required rate of return to reflect the implied bankruptcy or default risk whether a committed financial cash flows or returns from a commercial venture. This is obviously a purely precautionary approach aimed at circumventing premature commitments to risky transaction, but it is not an approach that tries to deal with the management of the underlying exposures per se. Trying to meaningfully determine a proper risk-adjusted discount rate, particularly in the context of cross-border investment decisions, is more an art that a pure science and a rather work-intense exercise compared to the potential outputs (e.g., Damodaran, 2010). In view of the difficulties to determine a proper discount rate in practice, many large seemingly sophisticated multinational firms tend to adhere to simpler payback analyses and use of relationship management as a way to deal with hard-to-quantify political risks in cross-border activities (Holmen and Pramborg, 2009).

In a seminal article, Myers (1977) demonstrated the need to generate cash flows for new investment opportunities as a necessary condition for optimal market valuation as the value of the firm is constituted by effective existing operations and the growth prospects of future business. In some ways, this resembles Ghoshal's (1987) focus on innovation in the multinational context as an important adaptive value enhancer to exploit emerging opportunities, where a too one-sided focus on operational efficiency can reduce flexibility and increase risk. Hence, the fundamental argument that changed things was the ability to make free cash flows and financial resources available to investment in profitable business propositions. Hence, Froot, Scharfstein and Stein (1993) argued that the ability to stabilize earnings, and dampen the volatility of operating cash flows, through risk management significantly reduces the likelihood of default, thereby both enhancing the availability of external funding and presumably at more favorable rates for investment purposes. This would also reduce the need to hold large liquidity and/or inventory buffers, thereby releasing free cash for better investment at higher returns (Merton, 2005). In addition, risk management can enhance the value-creating potential associated with unique firm-specific relationships, for example, with knowledgeable employees, specialized partner firms, and so on, as more stable business performance makes the firm a less risky counterpart (Wang, Barney, and Reuer, 2003; Andersen, 2008). Hence, any way risk management can increase incremental net cash inflows, extend the cash inflows in time, or reduce the riskiness of cash flows, the discounted cash flow model suggests that firm value is enhanced (Andersen, Garvey and Roggi, 2014). So, the first conundrum of modern finance theory (Bettis, 1983) seems to have been resolved, where the application of total risk management including major strategic exposures should be associated with handsome rewards to those that master the feat.

An operations management view

Operations management in an international organizational context deals with considerations around efficient supply chains that allow goods and services to be produced, delivered, and consumed by end-customers where they are located, at the time they need it, and in the proper quantities. This obviously can be disrupted by a variety of factors linked to resource access, input channels, production facilities, delivery systems, customer demands, and so on. This has spurred the development of business continuity planning frameworks and standards quite comparable to the emergence of various risk management frameworks, where operations obviously is an important element for the assessment of operational and infrastructure risks (e.g., BSI, 2007; FEMA, 2013). Cerulo and Cerulo (2004) note that business continuity planning often is characterized by ex post considerations as firms tend to establish disaster recovery plans after they have been affected by a disaster event. The contingency plans are typically focused on accidents and hazards and tend to address a relatively narrow set of risks that ignore serious threats. However, they find that organizations with business continuity planning have a higher likelihood of surviving major incidents (Cerulo and Cerulo, 2004).

Accordingly, Manuj and Mentzer (2008) point to weak-risk considerations around the design of supply chain networks and find that the study of risk management in global supply chains fail to take the various dimensions of risk into account. They suggest that effective operational risk management must have a risk management strategy that entails supply chain flexibility and assessment of environmental conditions (Manuj and Mentzer, 2008). This pinpoints a need for operational resilience, which means that an operating system is able to return to its original state, or move to a new, more desirable state after being exposed to one or more disruptions (Christopher and Peck, 2004). In other words, it opens not only for flexibility to redirect operating flows within an existing structure but also for the possibility of reorganizing the structure in ways that are better construed to deal with the changing context. Resilience reflects the ability to make positive adjustments under challenging conditions so the organization emerges stronger from those conditions, thereby displaying a capacity to face unexpected disruption, adapt, and persevere (Annarelli and Nonino, 2016). The resilience approach can engage resources across networked relationships to enable effective adaptation where many existing supply chain networks may be wanting. Hence, Rienkhemaniyom and Ravindran (2014) argue that a supply chain network design with a strong emphasis on optimization and profitability often includes inexpensive elements that reduce operational flexibility and thus represents a high disruption risk when conditions change. In this case, more attention should be given to gain a better balance between the trade-off choices of profits and disruption exposures when designing and structuring a supply chain network that is robust and resilient in a changing environment.

In other words, operational risks constitute an important part of the risk landscape as does the strategic risks that the risk management process attempts to identify in ex ante analyses of the major organizational exposures. However, seen from an ex post perspective, the experiences, particularly after the 2008 financial crisis, highlighted the fact that financial and economic exposures could become 'strategic' risks in the sense that they under extreme conditions might lead to life-threatening situations. So, an ex post perspective would analyze the ability to deal with all risks over a given time period as a measure of the effectiveness of 'total risk management' (e.g., Andersen, 2008). Andersen (2008) found that effective total risk management (including the handling of strategic exposures) is associated with superior performance, particularly in knowledge-based industries characterized by unique intangible assets, which is consistent with the firm-specific investment rationale. This rationale is grounded in the resource-based view of the firm and argues that key stakeholders engaged with the firm in unique relationships can generate incremental value, but in doing so reduce the flexibility of using their capabilities in other ways and configurations. In other words, these stakeholders increase their exposure to the firm. To entice stakeholders to remain engaged with the firm, using risk management to reduce the risk profile will make the firm a more credible counterpart (Wang et al., 2003). Further studies found that organizations with an emphasis on innovation investment as a means to explore alternative ways of moving forward experienced more positive total risk management effects (Andersen, 2009). Studies of the flexibility implied in multinational network structures found that the relationship between multinationality and risk outcomes (performance) to be negative (positive) but (inverse) U-shaped with the advantageous effects particularly displayed in knowledge-intensive businesses (Andersen, 2011, 2012).

Strategic risk management and ERM

In view of this, strategic risk management (SRM) – the ability to handle the total risk portfolio including strategic exposures – is different from the evolving concept of ERM. According to one of the leading ERM frameworks, COSO, ERM is a process to set a strategy across all activities in the enterprise designed to identify and manage potential events (risks) that may affect the organization. ERM is adopted with the aim of providing 'reasonable assurance' that the organization will achieve its objectives (COSO, 2004). In this way, the COSO framework is associated with a conventional view of strategy-making as strategic planning and subsequent strategy execution focused on four types of objectives:

achieve strategic goals, accomplish operational effectiveness, provide quality transparent reporting, and achieve compliance with all legal and policy requirements (COSO, 2004).

The strategic objectives of an organization are high-level goals aligned with the overarching mission and where strategic risks are those major internal and external events that can inhibit the achievement of those objectives. The strategic exposures are formed by those factors that represent the most consequential and significant risks to shareholder value or the value of the firm, so in this context SRM is seen as a critical element of ERM (Frigo and Anderson, 2001). According to this, the purpose of both SRM and ERM is to identify those risks that can inhibit the ability to achieve the strategic objectives set by the board, management, and others. This arguably requires a strategic view of the risk landscape that should be embedded in the strategy setting (implying a planning process) and strategy execution (implying subsequent implementation) and regular monitoring of key performance indicators (KPIs) related to the key strategic risks (COSO, 2004; Frigo and Anderson, 2001). The SRM function at LEGO is an example of integrated SRM based on principles of ERM and incorporating assessment of risks and opportunities in major investments using risk scenarios to prepare for uncertainty and support strategic decisions (Frigo and Læssøe, 2012).[1]

Nonetheless, a recent review of the history of the ERM approach concludes that "It can be argued that the ERM philosophy is flawed or that organizations have not implemented ERM effectively or a combination of the two" (McShane, 2018, p. 141). Similarly, Henriksen (2018) notes that ERM primarily focuses on strategy implementation and execution with little attention on emergent strategy development and therefore retains an emphasis on negative strategy outcomes as opposed to proactive risk-taking for future value-creation. He also observes that none of the companies in his study implement ERM to create value but rather to produce required documentation of risk management processes that tends to become bureaucratized in reality forming a 'paper tiger.' He concludes that the adoption of ERM frameworks in practice fails to link strategy-making to risk analysis but is instead motivated by compliance demands and external expectations (Henriksen, 2018).

Risk regulation and policy-making

The financial industry is of particular interest since many of the basic ideas behind the ERM concept to a large extent has been inspired by this sector and there is a high policy-making focus particularly with respect to regulating bank exposures that may point toward future developments. The Bank for International Settlements (BIS) as the global forum for banking regulators has been instrumental in developing common guidelines for proper risk handling in banks. As part of the Basel II guidelines initially published in 2004, the BIS introduced new approaches to consider exposures of operational risk and calculate capital buffers to circumvent potential impacts. In recent years, the BIS has realized that it is hard to identify and devise robust measures of operational exposures and possibly for that reason formal considerations for strategic exposures have only received peripheral mention.

In a keynote speech, Davis Carse (1999), the Deputy Chief Executive of the Hong Kong Monetary Authority, pointed to the importance of "electronic money products" and "electronic delivery channels" as affecting the competitiveness of conventional banking services. These represent strategic risks, that is, risks that the banks will not get it right by not making "the right choices when it comes to investing in e-banking" or by going down "a technological blind alley" (Carse, 1999). In another speech, Randall Kroszner (2008), member of the Board of Governors of the US Federal Reserve System, argued that financial services are in the midst of a fundamental transformation with potentially market-wide ramifications. He further argued that it "offers great potential opportunities for those institutions able to integrate strategy and risk management successfully" where survival hinges upon "integration in ... a 'strategic risk management framework.'" Despite these insightful contributions to the public debate, there has not yet been any suggestions from the BIS on how to construe such integrate SRM frameworks – one presumes because it is not so easy. The closest we get is a recommendation that the board should "approve and monitor the overall business strategy of the bank, taking into account the bank's long-term financial interests, its exposure to risk, and its ability to manage risk effectively" (BIS, 2015).

Nonetheless, (strategic) risk management is touted as linked to all aspects of business conduct and decision-making by examining both internal practices and the external environmental conditions they are faced with to understand the connection between the two (OECD, 2014). We see here the contours of a conventional strategic management approach as well as the basic principles of the ERM frameworks. The OECD (2014) argues that it is "generally accepted that boards should be responsible for setting a company's risk appetite or tolerance" and that it must be extended "to establishing and overseeing enterprise-wide risk management systems" (p. 16). So, while it is hard to identify and quantify strategic exposures, proponents still suggest formal requirements for enterprise-wide reporting of risk exposures. It is also now required that banks must have an independent risk management function directed by a chief risk officer (CFO) "with sufficient stature, independence, resources and access to the board" (OECD, 2014; BIS, 2015, p. 25). Meanwhile, there have been attempts in academia to quantify strategic risks resulting from "changes in strategic decisions and the business environment," including entry of new competitors or changes in customer demands (Chockalingam et al., 2018, p. 226). Yet, the purpose of evaluating the size of strategic exposures is to determine the amount of capital reserves the banks must allocate to cover the potential impacts from those events to avoid any larger systemic effects and repercussions for the general economy (Chockalingam et al., 2018). Hence, there are no considerations about how organizations can be more proactive in avoiding and/or dealing more effectively with these types potentially impactful strategic events.

The conceptualization of risk in the risk management frameworks (and their immediate origins) is a combination of probability and consequence of an identified event or particular set of circumstances with the purpose of minimizing negative and optimizing positive consequences and probabilities (ISO/IEC, 2002). It is claimed that "risk management is a central part of any organization's strategic management" that increases the probability of success and reduces the probability of failure and the uncertainty of achieving overall objectives (IRM, 2002, p. 12). Using the IRM (2002) standard as representative, the frameworks see strategy as concerned with long-term objectives, including capital availability, sovereign and political risks, legal and regulatory changes, environmental changes, stability of operations, and day-to-day delivery on objectives. This is consistent with the analytical approach of the conventional strategic management approach and also links to daily operations. There should be risk reporting to the board on significant exposures, business units should know their local risks, and people held accountable to report events quickly. The purpose is to create operational efficiency, effective internal controls, and compliance with laws and regulations. It is argued that "the Board has responsibility for determining the strategic direction of the organization and for creating the environment and the structures for risk management to operate effectively" (IRM, 2002, p. 12). In short, it is (almost) claimed that adoption of an ERM framework is a 'must' and will create value for the organization.

ERM as SRM

ERM is a broad conceptual framework that treats various risks in a holistic manner to manage *all* risks and their interactions with a reference to portfolio theory as a basis for managing the collective risks of the organization. It is a discipline to assess, control, exploit, finance, and monitor all identified risks with the intent to increase short- and long-term value for stakeholders (CAS, 2003). Operational risk is defined as the efficiency and reliability of assets and processes, and strategic risk is defined as fluctuations in demand and market prices, competition, regulatory and political issues, technology advances, and so on, much in line with environmental analysis as observed in the conventional strategic management approach. As no surprise then, there is a reference to establish the external context and hold it against the internal conditions in an SWOT analysis and assess both objectives and strategies devised to achieve them (CAS, 2003). Yet, there is a caveat connected to risk oversight and governance, namely that "not all enterprises are able to quantify intangible risks such as operational and strategic risk" (CAS, 2003, p. 33). We may wonder if this is related to the definitions of risk as identifiable events with quantifications of probability and impact. This approach can be very hard – maybe impossible – to apply in a meaningful way to (important) operational and strategic risks.

COSO (2004) argues that it is most critical for management to determine how much risk the organization is willing to accept to create value, which implicitly assumes a positive relationship between current risk-taking and future return. It is presented as an alignment between risk appetite and strategic decisions to enhance risk responses, seize opportunities, and improve the deployment of invested capital. Effective reporting and compliance is seen as the means to avoid reputational damage and provide reasonable assurance to the management and the board that objectives are achieved. There is one revelation, noting that "human judgement in decision making can be faulty" and "breakdowns can occur because of human failures" (COSO, 2004, p. 5), which is consistent with the research efforts attempting to identify the influence of different upper echelons theories on various strategic decision outcomes. Here, internal control is seen as an integral part of a safeguarded ERM system where everyone is assigned direct responsibility. COSO (2004) claims that "rule-making and other professional organizations providing guidance on financial management, auditing, and related topics should consider their standards and guidance in light of this framework" (p. 7). However, they do open for the possibility that the framework can be subjected to academic research and analysis. This obviously implies that most of the claims are made without support from empirical evidence, but is largely based on assumed effects and outcomes. We will discuss the empirical evidence in a later chapter.

A subsequent update (IRM, 2010) leans against the COSO (2004) and ISO31000 (2009) frameworks and claims that "risk management is an increasingly important business" and that "implementing a comprehensive approach will result in an organization benefiting from what is often referred to as the 'upside of risk'" (IRM, 2010, p. 2). These benefits are ascribed to successful risk management for compliance, assurance, and enhanced decision-making that leads to efficiency in operations, effective (change) tactics and strategy of the organization. It is claimed that "risk management is a central part of the strategic management of any organization" (IRM, 2010, p. 6) and that it is a continuous process to support the development and implementation of the strategy. While this sounds true, there is no prescription as to how this should be done, only more arguments that it 'must' be integrated with the organizational culture to promote operational efficiency at all levels.

A later update to COSO (2014) continues to see the implementation of ERM as a way to improve organizational performance and governance, claiming that "good risk management and internal control are necessary for long term success of all organizations" (p. 1). It presumes that organizational leaders articulate its objectives and develop strategies to achieve them, where risk management identifies the risks that may affect achieving those objectives and then mitigating them to reassure management and the board. This subscribes to the assumptions about a top-down–driven strategic thinking process to formulate the strategy where risk management then supports successful implementation to achieve objectives. This is pinpointed by arguing that governance starts with vision and mission and that strategy setting articulates a high-level plan to achieve one or more strategic goals, which clearly subscribes to the view of a traditional strategic planning process. It adds to this that it must include KPIs to establish management accountability and that it (somehow) can be translated into implemented changes to the corporate strategy and execution tactics (COSO, 2014). So, we observe a link to 'strategy setting' as a distinct view that the governance levels set a predetermined strategy and that the successful implementation must be achieved by holding individuals accountable for related KPIs. Hence, it is claimed that "the COSO frameworks contribute value to the overall governance and management processes" (COSO, 2014, p. 4).

COSO (2014) eloquently describes ERM as

> "a process, effected by an entity's board of directors, management
> and other personnel, applied in strategy-setting and across the en-
> terprise, designed to identify potential events that may affect the
> entity, to provide reasonable assurance regarding the achievement
> of entity objectives."
>
> (p. 4)

So, it is claimed to represent a management philosophy with shared
beliefs that the risk appetite statement frames the acceptable risk to
everyone in the organization and specifies the parameters to operate
within. This assumes that the top management echelons together with
the board of directors can predetermine the risk attitude of the organization so that all subsequent strategic and operational decisions
can take guidance and direction from this. However, we do not have
empirical evidence to show exactly how this takes place and indeed
whether it actually does take place in practice inside the organization
as expected in theory. It adds that "organizations must 'plan' for disruption and build and refine their radar systems to measure and be on
the alert for changes in key risk indicators" (COSO, 2014, p. 14). While
this sounds right and makes intuitive sense, it provides little guidance
as to what exactly that means and how it should be implemented into
practice.

A revised version of ISO 31000 (IRM, 2018) presents the ERM
framework as the means to create greater transparency and accountability where the corporate leadership must embrace opportunities and
think strategically about how to manage the increasing uncertainty,
complexity, and ambiguity of the world (IRM, 2018, p. 6). Again while
this sounds appealing and true, it does not provide much guidance as
to how exactly that is going to happen. It is added that it must consider
governance and culture, strategy and objective setting, performance,
information, communications, and reporting as a way of integrating
risk management into strategy and operational management. So, again
there is (also here) an emphasis integrating the strategy process with
risk management, but without explaining exactly how this should be
carried out. There is a note on the importance of human and cultural
factors, which is sensible given past experiences, but it probably needs
more specification as to what it means in practice to become truly help-
ful. The purpose of the ERM framework is to create and protect value
by managing risks, supporting decisions, setting strategy, and achieving objectives (IRM, 2018, p. 9). So, there continues to be an underlying

assumption about a top management governance-driven strategy setting process in line with a conventional strategic management view, although it is noted that integrated risk management follows a sequential structured process "in practice it is iterative" (IRM, 2018, p. 12). So, while strategy setting seems fairly linear and sequential, the risk management process is not, which bodes for more flexibility in interpreting the embedded processes, but also increases the level of confusion as to what and how things should be managed in practice.

Critique of ERM as SRM

The general principle behind ERM is the ability to identify potential risk events in advance and try to mitigate or transfer excessive exposure and manage the residual through different types of preparedness approaches. However, it is not possible to foresee all events, and uncertainty, by definition, cannot be predicted with any type of precision. So, given the turbulent business conditions, it is probably not advisable to be 100% dependent on ERM to do the job. Hence, Power (2009) argues that the design of the ERM approach is fundamentally flawed, because it is unable to deal with (true) uncertainty, articulate critical emergent risk events, and comprehend the unpredictable aspects of future risk scenarios. So, while the proponents of the ERM model do point to the need to identify unexpected events and take risks to embrace opportunities, the control-based foundation of the model prevents this from being accomplished. Instead, the well-intended aims of enterprise-wide risk handling may be burdened by implementation of highly formalized rule-based decision-making processes with audible documentation that creates (a large) bureaucracy and tends to automate risk responses (Power, 2004).

Add to this the potential for adverse effects from imposing 'stricter' risk management regulations (or reporting requirements) that 'cover the backs' of decision-makers and thereby may create a license to do more 'risky' things, as opposed to managing risk and uncertainty in a proactive manner. As Lam (2003, pp. 8–9), one of the early proponents of ERM, argued "perhaps the most compelling benefit of risk management is that it promotes job and financial security, especially for senior managers." In other words, the implantation of ERM and other legal/regulatory compliance approaches provides safety to engage in higher levels of risk-taking, or gambling, without engaging in considerations for innovative strategic responses to a changing competitive context.

Hence, a recent study by Pernell, Jung and Dobbin (2017) apply institutional theory of regulatory compliance and moral licensing in psychology to argue that implementation of formalized frameworks induced by policy-making and regulatory requirements can have unintended consequences. Stringent adherence to compliance may lead the way for champions of 'over-compliance' where an institutionalized feeling of 'good behavior' may reduce self-monitoring behavior within the organization. Hence, Pernell et al. (2017) find that executive compensation that promotes performance pay is associated with higher investment in (risky) financial derivatives as an indicator of increased risk-taking. That is, unbalanced compensation that rewards increasing share value, but without any punishment for drops in share value, leads to excessive risk-taking despite, or maybe because of, extensive formal frameworks and regulations. So, for example, the effects of the Sarbanes-Oxley Act of 2002, Basel II in 2004 with extended systems to manage operational risks (but few clues as to what it means), and ERM frameworks (COSO, 2004) could arguably legitimize higher risk-taking if proper risk governance is not in place.

Judging from the practice of ERM as it has evolved in the past, McShane (2018, p. 144) concludes that "the internal control/audit function is assuming a prominent role in ERM for many organizations." The initial definitions and updated descriptions of the ERM frameworks indicate a certain fluidity of the concept, which is partially a consequence of the complex inspiration from and relationship to the management control, internal audit, corporate finance, and governance fields. The academic research on ERM and its link to strategic management is still rudimentary and has mostly been published in accounting and finance journals and only rarely figure in management journals (Bromiley et al., 2014). There is an emerging consensus that both ERM and SRM should consider the total portfolio of risk that exposes the organization including operational and strategic risks that constitute the largest corporate exposures. Here the lack of relevant historical data prevents accurate measurement of risk effects and probabilities in empirical studies. There is also a sizeable literature linked to firm-specific risk management capabilities as a source of competitive advantage expressed in studies of dynamic capabilities (Teece et al., 1997; Teece, 2007), dynamic managerial capabilities (Adner and Helfat, 2003), and strategic response capabilities (Bettis and Hitt, 1995; Andersen et al., 2007). However, there is an apparent gap between the predominantly practice-based vocabulary of the ERM frameworks and the often theoretically founded capability studies where more fruitful research links between the two approaches are in short supply. The quantitative studies are affected by the limitation in calculated risk measures and qualitative studies uncover vastly different calculative behaviors in different organizations (Mikes, 2005, 2009). The ERM frameworks tend to adopt a particular view on the corporate strategy-making process where more nuance inspired by the strategy field could be useful. They also use vaguely defined constructs like 'risk appetite' and 'risk culture' where better definitions and evidence-based concepts can provide more productive conversations between scholars and practicing managers (Bromiley et al., 2014).

The connection between managerial assessments of risk and the application of standardized risk measures deserves more scrutiny as does the dynamics around interpersonal and interorganizational interpretations of identified risks and the implied effects on individual and group behaviors. What are the mental models adopted by organizational members related to the quantification and assessment of identified risks and does risk appetite and risk culture mean the same thing to different people in the organization? As a general conclusion, it seems evident that "the ERM field has taken a naïve view of organizational change" (Bromiley et al., 2014, p. 272) and therefore needs more attention. While this seems to be (partially) reflected in more updated versions of the major ERM frameworks (COSO, 2014; IRM, 2018), it is far from a concrete resolution and many questions remain open for further scrutiny and research. The majority of accounting and finance studies do not consider how the frameworks are implemented but readily assume that proposed objectives, reporting, and incentives lead to the proposed organizational practices and outcomes, where experience from practice tells us otherwise. The fact that the ERM frameworks make blatant claims about superior performance effects from formal risk management makes people believe that a control-based risk management approach can handle all the challenges of "increasing complexity and ambiguity" (IRM, 2018) when it most likely is not the case, and there is limited evidence to support the claims.

In conclusion, risk has been a central aspect of management, management accounting, strategy, and international business studies for a long time and has received specific attention in corporate finance, multinational financial management, and operations management as well. These diverse fields all cover different perspectives on the challenge of managing essential exposures in various business contexts. Particularly, the corporate finance field has formed some of the underpinning rationales behind the emergence of ERM aimed at optimizing resource allocation and achieving proper risk-adjusted returns across the entire business portfolio. The emergence of formal ERM approaches has been a significant development in risk management that opened the debate about possible differences between ERM and

SRM. Whereas ERM clearly is an integrative approach to deal with the total corporate risk portfolio, it is questioned whether ERM is able to address many of the strategic risks as effectively as it is claimed by some proponents. This contention continues to fuel the field and is addressed further in the ensuing chapters.

Note

1 It should be noted that this advanced ERM/SRM process is no longer applied as described within the LEGO Group.

3 Foundational studies

Risk is an inherent part of conducting business and arguably a critical aspect of the strategy-making process (Ruefli et al., 1999) and hence not surprisingly plays an important role in strategic management research (Bromiley, 1991; Pablo, Sitkin and Jemison, 1996). In financial economics and decision theory, risk has typically been conceived as and measured by the variance of realized financial returns over time (Ruefli et al., 1999). This way of looking at risk has been criticized among behavioral scholars as managers seem to associate risk more with the potential for downside losses than variance in outcomes (March and Shapira, 1987; Shapira, 1995). According to this, risk should be conceptualized as the expected deficiencies in performance compared to given aspirations (Miller and Leiblein, 1996). Ruefli et al. (1999) argue that the use of performance variance as a measure of risk lacks validity in a strategic management context and defines risk similar to behavioral scholars as "the probability of losing rank position vis a vis the other firms in the reference set" (1992, p. 1709). They further claim that previous research in strategic management "has been dominated by a few easy-to-calculate, borrowed measures of risk" that neglect the central concerns of strategic managers (Ruefli et al., 1999, p. 168). Gaining a better understanding of perceived risk and its role in organizations remains an important focus in strategic management (Miller and Leiblein, 1996; Pablo et al., 1996; Miller, Burke and Glick, 1998).

However, the attempts to study effects of risk in organizational settings have been hampered by confusion over different conceptualizations and measures of risk. In some cases, risk is conceived as an ex ante assessment of managerial choices with uncertain outcomes. Others characterize risk as an ex post phenomenon captured in the volatility of income flows over time. In strategic decision-making, risk usually arises because of these decisions, as they, by definition, involve uncertain outcomes that are important to long-term firm survival (Mintzberg, Raisinghani and Théorêt, 1976). Strategy scholars have long suggested a need to conceptualize risk from a strategic perspective (e.g., Bettis and Thomas, 1990; Ruefli, 1990; Bromiley, 1991). However, the terminology and definition of strategic risk has not yet found a consensus, and there is no clear distinction between use of the terms risk and uncertainty. Baird and Thomas (1985) were among the first scholars to consider the effects of strategic risk as those factors that relate to corporate strategic moves causing returns to vary and entailing uncertainty that could result in corporate ruin. This perspective is more akin to Frank Knight's (1921) concept of uncertainty as conditions with insufficient data available to make probabilistic predictions of future outcomes as opposed to risk for which realized events can be drawn from defined probability distributions.

Strategic risk

In the management literature, risk has often been used when referring to the potential *sources* of exposures in terms of external and/or internal factors that potentially have an impact on firm performance (Miller, 1992). From a strategic perspective, such events are often referred to as trends, developments, and environmental changes that may have an influence on the firm's long-term strategy (Ansoff, 1980; Dutton, Fahey and Narayanan, 1983), competitive advantage (Fiegenbaum and Thomas, 2004), and survival (Baird and Thomas, 1985; Slywotzky and Drzik, 2005). Slywotsky and Drzik (2005) base their considerations about the 'largest risks' by conceptualizing risk as a source of disruption defining strategic risk as the "array of external events and trends that can devastate a company's growth trajectory and shareholder value" (p. 80). They identify seven major types of strategic risks, including industry, technology, brand, competitor, customer, project, and stagnation. Andersen and Schrøder (2010) note that strategic risks typically derive from external factors such as competitor moves, new regulation, political events, social changes, change in customer taste, and new technologies. Bromiley, Rau and McShane (2016) highlight some concerns when risk is defined as sources of external factors since internal factors as well as the outcome of organizational choices must be considered. They further argue that it is problematic to define risk as trends, since it is only unpredictable trends that pose a significant exposure to the firm, so it is unexpected deviations from trends that constitute the actual risk.

March and Shapira (1987) note that "risk is most commonly conceived as reflecting variation in the distribution of possible outcomes, their likelihoods, and their subjective values" (p. 1404). In line with this, risk has been perceived as "the unpredictability in corporate outcome variables" (Miller, 1992, p. 312) and strategic decisions "for which the outcomes and probabilities may be only partially known" (Baird and Thomas, 1985, p. 231). In this sense, risk is embedded in organizational choices and outcomes from the (strategic) decisions made in firms. Others link strategic risk to decision-making and identify strategic risk by determining the degree of importance of the decision. Strategic risk then refers to the risk associated with factors that firms consider strategic (meaning important) and are related to those decisions that are taken at the top echelons of the organization. Johnson, Scholes and Whittington (2006) argue that "strategic risk can be seen as the probability and consequences of a failure of strategy" (p. 369). Among practice-based communities such as the Risk and Insurance Management Society (RIMS), strategic risk is interpreted as uncertainties and untapped opportunities that affect an organization's strategy and strategy execution (RIMS, 2011). This definition focuses on the strategic element of the definition rather than solely the 'risk' element. Yet, it does not distinguish between risk and uncertainty. It encompasses the potential situations where strategy formulation and the ensuing execution of that intended strategy can fail. That is, the risk of making the wrong choice by inadequately reflecting external and internal forces in the strategy deliberations or the failure of translating those strategic choices into the right actions to produce the right outcomes. Hence, it recognizes the risk that the strategic choice was inappropriate in the first place, for example, if an organization overinvests in a new product or pursues the wrong acquisition.

The most predominant enterprise risk management (ERM) frameworks recognize various risks as sourced by both external and internal factors and link their potential effects to the ability to reach the organization's strategic objectives. For example, COSO (2004, 2017) provides a definition of risk as the possibility that events will occur that can affect the achievement of strategic objectives. Likewise, ISO 31000 (2009, 2018) defines risk as the 'effect of uncertainty on objectives,' where the effect refers to the positive or negative deviation from what is expected. That is, the major ERM frameworks implicitly assume that the corporate governance level has determined a set of strategic objectives, where a structured approach to identify and manage major risk factors serves to enhance the ability to realize those strategic objectives. However, here again, there is no clear distinction between *risk* and uncertainty. Frigo and Anderson (2011) define strategic risk as those risks that are affected by both internal and external events and that potentially can inhibit an organization's ability to achieve its strategy and strategic objectives with the ultimate goal of creating and protecting shareholder and stakeholder value. Chatterjee et al. (2003) emphasize that managing strategic risk is a dynamic process where organizations identify and assess different obstacles that may influence or prevent the organization of realizing its financial and operational goals. This makes the definition of strategic risks dependent on the organization's predetermined reference points in the form of expressed intents, goals, and objectives and focuses risk management on the inability to achieve predefined expected targets. This can arguably be interpreted as a direct consequence of applying an accounting-driven blueprint of ERM grounded in a control-based approach to risk management. The implications are that these definitions do not confer to, or deal with, what Hirschborn (1999) calls primary risks, where an organization experiences ambiguity, drift, and an ongoing transformation of its core objectives.

Already in the 1980s, various management scholars coined the term of strategic issues, which in many respects are quite similar to the conceptualizations of strategic risk discussed above. Ansoff (1980) provided a first clear definition of strategic issue as "forthcoming developments, either inside or outside of the organization, which are likely to have an important impact on the ability of the enterprise to meet its objectives" (p. 132). Dutton and Duncan (1987b) take a somewhat broader approach and define strategic issues as "developments, events and trends having the potential to impact an organization's strategy" and note they can become "vehicles for translating individuals' concerns into organizational action" (p. 103). So, strategic issues are often ambiguous, complex and fluid, which makes their identification and diagnosis an ongoing interpretive and politically charged activity (Dutton, Fahey and Narayanan, 1983). A later definition by Dutton and Dukerich (1991) highlights the importance of the cognitive mental processes that are involved when (strategic) decision-makers deal with major issues. This leads to a narrower more confined definition of strategic issues as "events, developments, and trends that an organization's members collectively recognize as having some consequence to the organization" and they "can arise from change inside or outside of the organization" (Dutton and Dukerich, 1991, p. 518). Similar to Ansoff (1980), this later definition recognizes that strategic issues can be emerging opportunities in the external environment or an internal strength to be exploited, as well as an external environmental threat or an internal organizational weakness. Dutton and Duncan (1987a) provide an example of a 'threat' issue as when a competitor introduces a new technology or product that substantially modifies the availability of substitutes, and poses a significant threat to the viability of a firm's existing product.

They also stress that 'opportunity' issues represent developments or trends that if acted upon may provide a potential gain to the organization and might become a major competitive advantage for a firm (Dutton and Duncan, 1987a). King (1982) provides the working definition of strategic issues as a 'condition' or 'pressure' on the organization that may have an impact on firm performance, may lead to controversy among decision-makers, and may result in different strategies to be implemented. Accordingly, Ansoff (1980) also introduced the concept of a 'key strategic issue list,' which is the listing of key issues the organizations is facing at a given point in time. This is quite akin to the notion of maintaining a register of 'strategic risks' identified, managed, and monitored for strategic management purposes. Dutton and Duncan (1987a) extend this notion by discussing a concept of 'strategic issue array,' defined as the set of strategic issues identified, discussed and prioritized by the top management team. The strategic issue array emerges as a result of a strategic planning process and contains the issues that affect the implementation of strategic change initiatives. Hence, it could be argued that the discussion of 'strategic issues' as potential effects from within or from outside the organization constitute factors of significant importance to key decision-makers and as such constitute precursors to later definitions of strategic risk.

Managing strategic risk

According to Gavetti et al. (2005, p. 691), "strategy-making is most critical in times of change and in unfamiliar environments" pointing to a major area of research in the strategy field, namely, how firms can sustain competitive advantage in changing environments (Barney, 1991). To sustain their competitive position, the firms must develop adaptive capabilities that identify emergent strategic risks and generate appropriate strategic responses (Andersen et al., 2007). These responses could imply substantial strategic risk-taking in attempts to replace obsolete source endowments (Chatterjee et al., 2003), implying significant uncertainty and downside exposure that might erode firm value (Bettis and Hitt, 1995). Hence, while engaging in strategic risk-taking, a related challenge for firms is to limit the downside risk of these moves while capturing the upside gains.

In the 1980s, a dominant view in management on successful strategies assumed that decision-makers base their decisions on rationality supported by comprehensive and exhuastive analysis (Hart, 1992). The rationality assumption implies that "a decision maker considers all available alternatives, idenitifes and evaluates all of the consequences which would follow from adoption of each alternative and selects the alternative that would be preferable in terms of the most values ends" (Hart, 1992, p. 328). This means that all other things being equal organizations make the same strategic decisions and the process of strategic management is rational and formal (Mintzberg et al., 1998). Based on this logic, strategic planning has since the earliest foundations of strategic management been conceived as an important tool to manage environmental developments and the strategic exposures that come with these changes (Boyd, 1991). Today, strategic planning is one of the most widely used strategy practices within firms (Whittington, 2006; Spee and Jarzabkowski, 2011). Strategic planning has been described as the organizational process of developing a firm's mission, long-term objectives, and the plans to attain them, as well as the ongoing system that monitors the achievement of the strategic objectives (e.g., Andrews, 1971; Cohen and Cyert, 1973; Ansoff, 1988; Boyd and Reuning-Elliott, 1998).

Much of the empirical research on the relationship between strategic planning and firm performance has been inconclusive, not least in studying the relationship under the contingency of risk and uncertainty. Some studies have concluded that there is no clear systematic relationship between strategic planning and organizational performance (Scott, Mitchell and Birnbaum, 1981; Shrader, Taylor and Dalton, 1984). Various later studies that define strategic planning as a rational analytical strategy-making approach find positive relationships to performance, particularly in dynamic environments (Miller and Cardinal, 1994; Brews and Hunt, 1999; Andersen, 2000; O'Regan, Sims and Gallear, 2008). However, the positive performance outcomes seem to apply specifically to organizations that are able to engage in both central and decentralized strategy-making at the same time (Banbury and Hart, 1994; Brews and Hunt, 1999; Andersen, 2004).

The strategy field has engaged in a debate about whether strategy-making takes place through formal deliberate planning processes or they emerge as a firm muddles through and learns from changing conditions by trial and error. The former approach advocates a rational systematic planning process (Schendel and Hofer, 1979; Ansoff, 1988), whereas the latter school supports emergent processes (Mintzberg, 1978; Mintzberg and Waters, 1982). The planning school emphasizes the positive aspects of strategic planning where careful analysis can articulate a unifying strategic direction where integration and coordinated efforts enhance efficiency and firm performance (Ansoff, 1984; Greenley, 1994). The emergence school questions the assumption that firms can prepare for an uncertain future through rigorous analysis and stresses that planning can lead to increased bureaucracy and rigid structures. It is further stressed that a top-down strategy-making approach is inadequate in detecting, interpreting, and handling strategic risks. Rather, organizations need to "discover how to tap people's commitment and capacity to learn at *all* levels" (Senge, 1990, p. 4). Hence, the strategic management literature has placed emphasis on the role of middle managers when dealing with changing environments and when responsiveness, flexibility, and the ability to capture emergent opportunities are important for firm survival (e.g., Kanter, 1982; Burgelman, 1983; Pascale, 1984; Wooldridge and Floyd, 1990; Bower and Noda, 1996). Due to their proximity to the actual activities and operations, middle managers often have a unique knowledge of strategic risk exposures, such as market developments, shifts in customer demands, and competitor moves (Kanter, 1982; Pascale, 1984; Wooldridge and Floyd, 1990; Mahnke, Venzin and Zahra, 2007). This has led to an increased call for a decentralized strategy-making.

On the other hand, Grant (2003) stresses that the debate between the two (seemingly opposing) schools of thought is based on a misconception of the real activities in the strategic planning process. In his study of strategy-making among major oil companies, he found that strategic planning can be described more as a process of planned emergence. He stresses that "uncertainty requires that strategy is concerned less with specific actions and the more with establishing clarity of direction within which short-term flexibility can be reconciled with overall coordination of strategic decisions" (Grant, 2003, p. 493). The primary strategic direction of the firm was derived from decisions made by managers located below the top management level, where the strategic planning activities coordinated and improved the quality of those strategic decisions (Grant, 2003). Along the same lines, Wolf and Floyd (2013) note that "the purpose of strategic planning is to influence an organization's strategic direction for a given period and to coordinate and integrate deliberate as well as emerging strategic decisions" (p. 5). Similarly, Andersen and Nielsen (2009) show how strategic emergence is derived from responsive actions taken by empowered managers, which in turn is positively mediated by strategic planning to achieve superior performance.

This suggests that strategic planning can play an important role as an integrative device that coordinates strategic initiatives and builds a shared strategic understanding or particular state of mind

(Ohmae, 1982; Ketokivi and Castañer, 2004; Andersen and Nielsen, 2009) and provide top managers with a sense of direction and control (Falshaw, Glaister and Tatoglu, 2006). These studies indicate that strategic planning as a rational analytical approach to strategy-making acts as an important mediating mechanism between decentralized emerging initiatives and the effective realization of strategic outcomes (Andersen and Nielsen, 2009) building on the cognitive diversity of top management (Miller, Burke and Glick, 1998) and organizational risk awareness (O'Regan, Sims and Gallear, 2008). Indeed, it appears from the empirical evidence that the conventional strategic management model, which is largely commensurate with strategic planning, has important (direct and mediating) effects on the way firms can deal with and manage their strategic exposures. This does not imply that we must choose between strategy-making through planning or emergence, both aspects are important as emergent autonomous initiatives can generate effective strategies supported by planning (Andersen and Nielsen, 2009). It is further argued that a strategy-making process where autonomous initiatives and strategic planning interact over time is a key characteristic of adaptive organizations (Andersen, 2015).

Strategic risks and strategic issues

As discussed in the previous section, the early strategy literature conceived of an organization's (identified and emergent) strategic exposures using a slightly different terminology by referring to strategic issues as opposed to strategic risks. Igor Ansoff, a proponent of strategic planning, was one of the first strategy scholars to develop a systematic approach for early identification and fast responses to manage strategic issues, referred to as a strategic issue management system (Ansoff, 1980). In a review of the literature, Dutton and Ottensmeyer (1987) define the concept as a "set of organizational procedures, routines, personnel, and processes devoted to perceiving, analyzing, and responding to strategic issues; they enhance an organization's capacity to adapt and to learn" (p. 355). It is argued that strategic issue management systems can overcome the limitations of the periodic strategic planning process by responding to emergent environmental signals in real time (Ansoff, 1980). Including ongoing strategic issue identification can be incorporated as a mechanism to challenge the current strategy and engage in regular strategy revision exercises outside a calendar determined by the planning cycle (King, 1982). A strategic issue management system involves continuous monitoring and early detection of important trends and developments that enable an updated understanding of the changing competitive context and its strategic implication taking proper measures to respond in a timely manner. Fahey and King (1977) emphasize that timely responses to real-time emergent strategic issues requires formal responsibility and accountability to a scanning function with formal channels for information-sharing with an explicit linkage to the strategic planning process. In this model, an official scanning function can support the ongoing creation of "variety of choices inherent in strategic planning" (Fahey and King, 1977, p. 63).

While much of the strategy literature has focused on the implications for firm performance, a number of studies specifically look at risk outcomes. For example, Sheehan (1975) studied how strategic planning relates to or influences fluctuations in performance outcomes. Capon, Fakley and Hulbert (1994) and Delmar and Shane (2003) find that engaging in a strategic planning process increases the likelihood of the survival of the firm as an independent entity, which represents a particularly important type of risk-related outcomes. The scholarship around prospect theory (Kahneman and Tversky, 1979; Voss, Sirdeshmukh and Voss, 2008) and the threat rigidity literature (Staw, Sandelands and Dutton, 1981; Sitkin and Pablo, 1992) has studied how risk may affect management choice and managerial practices and behaviors, but there is a shortage of studies on how strategy-making practices affect risk outcomes. Bromiley (1991) studied the relationship between risk-taking and economic performance, and vice versa, as critical issues in strategic management and found that performance seems to decrease risk-taking while risk-taking leads to lower performance in line with the Bowman paradox (Bowman, 1980, 1984). Risk-taking has typically been measured by variance in predicted or realized performance reflecting variance in returns or income streams as common risk indicators (e.g., Bettis and Mahajan, 1985; Bromiley, 1991; Wiseman and Bromiley, 1996). More analyses using proper risk measures as explanandum (as well as explanaans) can help provide better guidance to risk management practice and generate further theory-building about the effects of various practices, processes, and tools applied in strategic (risk) management.

Managing strategic risks with control systems

The management accounting literature has pointed to different internal control systems as the means to monitor and handle strategic risk exposures. Control systems are conceived as formalized routines and procedures that use (hopefully updated) information to change patterns in organizations activity (Simons, 1987). These systems gather information to evaluate organizational performance (e.g., financial, operational efficiency, capabilities, human resources, risk exposures) in view of strategic goals, objectives, targets, and risk limits. Similar to strategic planning, the control systems have been described as practices concerned with reporting to adapt the organization, making sure that organizational objectives are met (Horngren, Foster and Datar, 1994; Kloot, 1997).

In 1992, the Commission Committee of Sponsoring Organizations of the Treadway Commission (COSO), a coalition of the main accounting and finance trade associations in the USA, published the standard for best practice in designing internal control systems with the title: Internal Control—Integrated Framework. The framework identifies risk management as one of five elements in a control system. The original focus of COSO was not on risk per se, but tried to uncover the causes behind the internal control problems that contributed to major financial reporting failures in the late 1970s and 1980s (Moeller, 2007). Yet, it provided the conceptual building block for the ERM framework COSO published in 2004. The standard complemented the Sarbanes-Oxley Act (SOX) of 2002, which was a direct response to the major corporate scandals of WorldCom and Enron.

The COSO (2004) framework was drafted by engaged consultants from PricewaterhouseCoopers specifically aimed to develop a framework that would enable managers to evaluate and improve organizational risk management systems. Hence, the focus shifted from risk management as a component of internal control to one in which risk management effectively encompassed the principles of internal controls. This formed a focus on the ERM frameworks that "can be traced to an accounting conception of internal control" (Power, 2009, p. 850). While other risk management frameworks appeared in the early 2000s, the COSO standard has arguably become the most widely used risk management framework in North America (with strong influences in Europe as well) and has been described as "a world-level template for best practice" (Power, 2007, p. 849).

The motivation for ERM

The failures of traditional or corporate risk management in spectacular and devastating cases, such as Enron, WorldCom, and Lehman Brothers, urged regulators, stock exchanges, institutional investors, and corporate governance oversight bodies to put pressure on top management to take responsibility for managing risk on an enterprise-wide scale (CAS, 2003). Hence, the concept of ERM arose as an extension to traditional risk management (TRM) as it was practiced during the

1990s. The focus of TRM was primarily linked to managing hazards and financial risks that were commonly managed by separate insurance and financial market entities located in 'silos' with little interaction between them. ERM was intended to circumvent the observed limitations of TRM, for example, by failing to see possible relationships between risks and reducing excessive administrative costs from separate insurance and risk management functions (Alviunessen and Jankensgard, 2009). Oversight of new or emergent risks might fall between the functional silos and be neglected in the corporate risk profile, leading to inappropriate or inconsistent decision-making across departments and business entities (Nielson, Kleffner and Lee, 2005).

Recognizing these limitations, a number of risk management frameworks were developed by different professional associations, advisory, and standard setting bodies adopting a variety of approaches to the definition and implementation of ERM. Accordingly, Power (2007) claims that ERM can be seen as an 'umbrella concept' where organizations cannot assume reference to a coherent set of practices. In studies of risk management practices in the implicated financial industry, other researchers found ERM to be an elusive and rather under-specified concept (Mikes, 2005). Part of the explanation for these observations may be found in the diversity of definitions of ERM and descriptions of practices presented by different institutions (see Table 3.1).

Despite the differences in definitions and terminologies applied to ERM in the various frameworks (Table 3.1), there seems to be a general consensus about some of the core elements of the ERM frameworks, for example, they should:

- Manage *all* risks including nonfinancial risks such as strategic and operational risks;
- Include both the *upside* potentials of risk and the *downside* losses;
- Adopt an enterprise-wide approach looking across the entire portfolio of risks spanning *all* functions, business units, and divisions.

The frameworks implicitly, and often also explicitly, include considerations about strategic risks as being part of the concerns in ERM. For example, COSO's definition specifically highlights that ERM is a process applied to strategy settings. The frameworks also stress the upside opportunity dimension of various risks. So, rather than using risk management as a defensive mechanism to (only) protect against downside loss, with the purpose of minimizing or avoiding risk, organizations should recognize the opportunistic side of risk management and the potential value of risk-taking. Firms with a unique

Table 3.1 Different conceptualizations of enterprise risk management (ERM)[1]

Casualty Actuarial Society (2003)	ERM is the process by which organizations in all industries assess, control, exploit, finance, and monitor risks from all sources for the purpose of increasing the organization's short- and long-term value to its stakeholders.
Institute of Risk Management (IRM) Risk Management Standard (2002)	ERM is a central part of any organization's strategic management. It is the process whereby organizations methodically address the risks attaching to their activities with the goal of achieving sustained benefit within each activity and across the portfolio of all activities.
COSO (2004)	ERM is a process, affected by an entity's board of directors, management and other personnel, applied in strategy setting and across the enterprise, designed to identify potential events that may affect the entity, and manage risk to be within its risk appetite, to provide reasonable assurance regarding the achievement of entity objectives.
AS/NZS 4360 (2004)	Risk management is the culture, processes, and structures that are directed toward the effective management of potential opportunities and adverse effects.
S&P (2008)	ERM is an approach to assure the firm is attending to all risks; a set of expectations among management, shareholders, and the board about which risks the firm will and will not take; a set of methods for avoiding situations that might result in losses that would be outside the firm's tolerance; a method to shift focus from "cost/benefit" to "risk/reward"; a way to help fulfill a fundamental responsibility of a company's board and senior management; a toolkit for trimming excess risks and a system for intelligently selecting which risks need trimming; and a language for communicating the firm's efforts to maintain a manageable risk profile.
ISO31000 (2009)	Risk management is coordinated activities to direct and control an organization with regard to risk.
RIMS (2011)	ERM is a strategic business discipline that supports the achievement of an organization's objectives by addressing the full spectrum of its risks and managing the combined impact of those risks as an interrelated risk portfolio.
COSO (2017)	The culture, capabilities, and practices, integrated with strategy setting and performance, that organizations rely on to manage risk in creating, preserving, and realizing value.

capability for managing a particular (strategic) risk should seek competitive advantage from it and not just consider risk as a problem to mitigate (Bromiley et al., 2016). The ERM frameworks represent a portfolio approach to manage the totality of risks faced by a firm (Dickinson, 2001). This portfolio thinking has drawn inspiration from modern portfolio theory, with underlying assumptions that a portfolio of risk is not the simple sum of the individual risk elements and that to understand the aggregated risk – one must understand the individual risk elements plus their interactions. Hence, the portfolio of risk, or the aggregated risk of the entire organization, is a relevant consideration when managing the major corporate risks that face an organization (CAS, 2003). Another common denominator of the frameworks is that organizations should apply a systematic approach to risk management by identifying, assessing, evaluating, responding, and reporting all risks (opportunities and threats) that can affect the organization (IIA, 2009). These core activities are executed in systematic processes with standardized procedures across the organization (Moeller, 2007).

The ERM frameworks are now broadly regarded as the best practice for risk management, governance, and good management (Fraser, Schoening-Thiessen and Simkins, 2008). Hence, applying ERM is trying to signal sound corporate governance where firms as a consequence may put themselves at risk by disregarding its application (Martin and Power, 2007). The major credit-rating agencies Fitch, Moody's and Standard & Poor's (S&P) include 'management and governance' as part of their rating of organizational credit worthiness, which encompasses assessments of the comprehensiveness of the enterprise-wide risk management system and the effectiveness of board risk oversight. S&P formally evaluate ERM in all its management and governance assessments. According to S&P, "corporate enterprises with a deliberate, consistent, articulated, resourced, and integrated approach that effectively identifies, selects, and prudently mitigates risks are more likely to build long-term credit strength as compared to enterprises with a casual, opportunistic, or reactive approach" (S&P, 2012, p. 10).

The benefits of adopting ERM processes are supposed to accrue from more efficient and consistent risk management processes that enhanced firm value and performance (Barton, Shenkir and Walker, 2002; Lam, 2003; Gordon, Loeb and Tseng, 2009; Hoyt and Liebenberg, 2011). Nonetheless, the empirical evidence remains rather inconclusive on this matter. The 'obscureness' and inconsistent applications of the ERM concept in the research literature might partially explain the mixed findings (Kraus and Lehner, 2012) as well as the relationship between ERM and firm performance may be contingent on unidentified internal conditions. For example, Gordon et al. (2009) provide empirical evidence that firm size, organizational complexity, and encouragement by the board of directors constitute key internal contingencies that affect the relationship between ERM and firm performance. Other researchers have proposed that aspects of leadership style, such as, encouraging people to speak up and report on risk events and imposing a culture that does not penalize or blame but reward such behavior, are highly important contextual factors to ERM's success (Spedding and Rose, 2008; Mikes and Kaplan, 2014).

So far, the literature has not been able to adequately address the impact of corporate culture on ERM implementation and practices (Fraser et al., 2008). Overall, the shortcomings in exploring risk management processes from a strategic management perspective have been accentuated by a number of scholars (Chatterjee et al., 2003; Power, 2007). Hence, Bromiley et al. (2014) assert that "regrettably, the evolving discussion about ERM has not been informed by relevant work in management on risk, strategic management, organizational change and other relevant topics" (p. 265). Since the current literature on ERM to a large extent has been influenced by the management accounting and auditing fields as well as the risk management practitioner literature (Bromiley et al., 2014), there is a strong tendency to frame ERM as a traditional control system. However, recent shifts in this perspective stress that the value-creating potential of ERM can only be observed if it is integrated into the organization's strategy-making processes (Andersen, 2008; Frigo and Anderson, 2001; Beasley, Branson and Pagach, 2015; Sax and Andersen, 2018).

ERM versus strategic risk management

Proponents of ERM have been advocating the integration of ERM with strategic planning (e.g., Moeller, 2007; Fraser and Simkins, 2009; Frigo and Anderson, 2001; Beasley, Branson and Pagach, 2015). Beasley and Frigo (2010) argue that critical 'blind spots' in the execution of a strategy can be overlooked if risk management is not linked to the strategic planning process. This view implies a conventional top-down strategy-making process, which is expressed in the updated ERM frameworks (COSO, 2017; ISO, 2018), is expressed by claiming that ERM is related to strategy setting. ERM users have nonetheless voiced frustrations about how to implement these aspects as there is little specific guidance on how to exploit the upside potential of risk and how risk management is involved in the formation and implementation of strategy. Hence, the strategic planning and ERM processes have remained disintegrated in most organizations managed in separate organizational silos. A survey of corporate risk managers by RIMS in 2011 revealed that four in ten organizations did not have formal processes in place to align risk management with corporate strategy. Beasley, Branson and Hancock (2012, 2016)[2] find that the number of firms that feel unable to integrate ERM and strategic management have increased from 33% to 56% over the four-year period 2012–2016. This suggests that organizational processes to develop business planning and managing risk are separated and indicate a tendency to consider risk strategies after the business strategies have been decided. Maybe not surprisingly, Beasley et al. (2015) find that the perception of ERM as an important tool for strategy setting is higher in organizations that have articulated a formal risk appetite in the context of the strategic planning process. One reason for these results arguably is that ERM primarily considers the reporting aspects of an internal control framework focused on compliance rather than providing insights in support of setting and achieving strategic objectives. Partially in response to these concerns, COSO released the updated version of the ERM framework in 2017, now entitled "Enterprise Risk Management – Integrating with Strategy and Performance," to highlight the importance of considering risk both in strategy setting and driving performance. The ISO 31000 ERM framework was similarly updated in 2018 to provide more concise guidance and help organizations use risk management to integrate the ERM principles into all activities, including strategy and planning, governance, compliance, business continuity, and crisis management.

The updated COSO 2017 framework has, among other things, refined the definition of ERM to be more focused on strategy integration: "ERM is the culture, capabilities, and practices, integrated with strategy setting and performance, that organizations rely on to manage risk in creating, preserving, and realizing value." It has also responded to one of the key flaws in the initial framework, suggesting that objectives are to be irrevocably set prior to the identification of the events that could disrupt the achievement hereof as opposed to an approach where different strategies are considered in light of identified risks. Further, the framework has been updated to consider strategy and objective setting as something that occurs multiple times throughout different stages, as opposed to being a one-time event (Pierce and Goldstein, 2018). Future research could examine whether the updated framework suggesting changes to the use of ERM in organizations will in effect contribute to more integrated processes between ERM and strategy-making.

Managing strategic risks through interactive controls

The defintions of ERM (Table 3.1) have much resemblance to Anthony's (1965) widely quoted definition of management control as "the process by which managers ensure that resources are obtained and used effectively and efficiently in the accomplishment of the organization's objectives" (p. 17). Firms use management control systems to communicate the strategy to employees by setting targets, developing metrics for monitoring, and aligning the incentive structure. These control systems have traditionally been backward-looking and used to monitor development toward set objectives and reward achievement of specified goals and targets in regular reviews of critical performance variables, or key success factors (KPIs). This application can typically be found in the way budget systems, balanced scorecards, and project management systems are construed following the principles of diagnostic control. The implied control process in strategic planning follows a similar pattern of periodic reporting of deviations from the planned outcomes to inform top management and the board. However, parts of the management accounting literature have criticized this type of control system for being inadequate in terms of managing strategic risks in dynamic environments that require flexibility and innovation (Simons, 1995b).

Some scholars argue that diagnostic control systems are incomplete and fail to produce adequate updated information and are, therefore, considered untimely and at times unreliable (e.g., Burns and Vaivio, 2001). Instead, firms should use control systems interactively that according to Simons (1994) "enables top-level managers to focus on strategic uncertainties, to learn about threats and opportunities as competitive conditions change, and to respond proactively" (p. 81). Using control systems interactively "build internal pressure to break out of narrow routines, stimulate opportunity seeking and encourage the emergence of strategic initiatives as future states are re-estimated" (Bruining, Bonnet and Wright, 2004, p. 158). Interactive controls enable top managers "to regularly and personally involve themselves in the decision activities of subordinates" (Simons, 1994, p. 171). While diagnostic control systems assist organizations in the pursuit of intended strategic goals, interactive use of control systems focuses on strategic uncertainties and creates a pressure to find innovative solutions in response to identified strategic exposures. Thus, interactive control systems are central to strategy formation as they may manage the emergence of strategic responses (Simons, 1991, 1994; Marginson, 2002). Nonetheless, the relationship between strategy-making and control systems remains a largely unexplored area of strategic management (Marginson, 2002; Kober, Ng and Paul, 2007).

Simons (1995a, b) suggests that interactive control systems make up one of four levers of control that affect business activities, where the other three are boundary systems, belief systems, and diagnostic control systems. Together, these four levers of control can work as part of the organizational strategy-making process as a way to balance between creativity and control (Simons, 1994; Chenhall, 2003; Widener, 2007). The belief and boundary systems articulate limits for strategic risk-taking and inform organizational members about what types of strategic opportunities to explore and exploit (Roberts, 1990; Simons, 1994; Widener, 2007). The belief system represents the basic values and purpose of the firm as communicated formally by the top management (Simons, 1995a). This serves to secure goal commitment throughout the organization and inspire employees in their search for opportunities and business responses without prescribing the nature of activities in detail (Tuomela, 2005). The boundary system communicates the domain of acceptable activities to ensure effective resource utilization. Thus, a boundary system should form an understanding of acceptable risks and business activities to be avoided altogether (Simons, 1994; Tuomela, 2005). For all intents and purposes, these control systems are commensurate with those elements of the strategic planning process that lay out the firm's mission statement typically consisting of an overarching purpose, long-term goals, and an outline of corporate values with prioritized behaviors (e.g., Boyd and Reuning-Elliott, 1998). Accordingly, Porter (1996) argues that it is as important to determine which type of businesses not to engage in as it is to decide in the strategic planning process what activities one should pursue going forward. Thus, strategic planning is itself a form of control process providing directions and setting boundaries for managerial decisions.

Diagnostic control systems monitor the achievement of predetermined strategic actions and results in accordance with presumed performance standards. For example, budget systems are typically used to assess expected outcomes of the strategic plan for the coming accounting year as the basis for resource allocation and monitoring of business units and their managers. In general, budgets serve as a medium to quantify outcomes of the long-term strategic plan with a focus on a single year (Otley, 1999; Hofmann, Wald and Gleich, 2012). The completion of budgets provides a means to communicate critical performance variables and subsequently monitor the implementation of the intended strategic aims. In that sense, budgets provide implied direction toward achieving predetermined strategic goals by focusing on established targets and correcting deviations from that path (Hofmann et al., 2012). In the strategy literature, this is referred to as strategic control and is considered part of the strategic planning process (Lorange, 1977; Schendel and Hofer, 1979; Schreyogg and Steinmann, 1987; Goold and Quinn, 1990).

Hence, the strategic planning process effectively incorporates central elements of the belief, boundary, and diagnostic control systems (Simons, 1994). Since realized outcomes often differ from the plans, the strategic control may provide some learning about changing environmental conditions and the related means-ends relationships although this can be exceedingly difficult in uncertain environmental contexts (Goold and Quinn, 1990; Quinn, 1996). Under these conditions, diagnostic controls have been criticized for constraining the operational flexibility of autonomous managers in ways that inhibit collaborative cross-functional initiatives, innovation, and creativity (Frow, Marginson and Ogden, 2010). More specifically, it has been argued that traditional strategic planning and budgeting processes "force managers at all levels to commit to delivering specified outcomes, even though many of the variables underpinning those outcomes are beyond their control" (Hope and Fraser, 2003, p. 18). So, in turbulent environmental contexts, these processes may constrain responsiveness and create a "performance trap" (ibid).

Turbulent environmental conditions are subjected to high levels of strategic risks where interactive rather than diagnostic control systems are considered the most effective way to handle the implied exposures (Simons, 1994; Marginson, 2002). Interactive control systems are used to generate dialog, idea generation, and learning rather than control at-a-distance through automatic processes (Burchell et al., 1980; Simons, 1994). This interactive dimension constitutes a distinct mechanism not considered in strategic control as part of the conventional strategic planning model. Interactive control systems involve frequent face-to-face dialogues between top management and lower level managers, where the information is shared openly across management levels and functions. Furthermore, the interaction requires a noninvasive, facilitating, and inspirational involvement of top management (Simons, 1994). Interactive controls can thus become a pertinent vehicle for the exchange of updated information about emergent strategic exposures that facilitate organizational learning by involving managers at different hierarchical levels in the forward-looking analytical considerations as well as engaging in retrospective discussions about experiential insights gained from low-level initiatives.

Hence, the process goes beyond internal control and entails

"not only participation between subordinates and superiors in (for example) the budget setting, but also an ongoing dialogue between organizational members as to why budget variances occur, how the system or behaviors can be adapted and even whether any actions should be taken in response to these variances."

(Abernethy and Brownell, 1999, p. 191)

Although Simons (1995b, p. 122) highlights that middle managers are "important in making interactive control processes work effectively" as they are "key nodes of the information networks that reveals senior management's concern," the interactive control systems do not imply managerial autonomy per se. In fact, interactive control systems and increased flexibility from dispersed decision rights are not antithetical but mutually compatible (Gul and Chia, 1994; Simons, 1994; Marginson, 2002). The attention is restrained to the top management level, and Simons (1994) acknowledges that interactive processes can be applied to all organizational levels, although this view of an interactive use is not the focus of his analysis. In this way, the strategic planning process, decentralized strategy-making, and interactive controls are three distinct but complementary components of an integrative strategy model.

Empirical research has shown a positive direct effect of interactive control systems on strategic change (Abernethy and Brownell, 1999; Naranjo-Gil and Hartmann, 2007), innovativeness, and learning (Henri, 2006). Naranjo-Gil and Hartmann (2007) also found that interactive use of controls and the extent of change was more positive for prospector firms than defender firms. Accordingly, Bisbe and Otley (2004) emphasize that innovation risk is managed more effectively by interactive systems, and they found that interactive control systems moderate the impact of innovation on performance. In a study of the link between interactive controls and strategy-making, Widener (2007) found that interactive control was used to scan the external environment, which enhances performance through an increased attention span. However, in contrast to the proposed framework, she did not find evidence that interactive controls enhance organizational learning.

In essence, the interactive control systems encourage debate about strategic goals and targets in face-to-face discussions with top management that allow subordinates to challenge prevailing assumptions and action plans (Simons, 1994). It can thus play an important role in extending opportunity seeking behaviors and collective learning throughout the organization where new strategies can emerge from the process (Henri, 2006). In particular, "interactive control systems are essential to monitor competitive risk in a culture that could potentially create barriers to impede the free flow of information about emerging threats and opportunities" (Simons, 2000, p. 261). In that way, interactive controls can help top managers learn about strategic risks and respond proactively to these emergent exposures by breaking out of narrow search routines (Simons, 1994).

Mikes (2009) has investigated the diagnostic applications of the formal risk management systems or frameworks and claims that strategic risk management (SRM) can be conceived as a risk management systems being used interactively. These are the risk management systems that management actively draws upon as they shape important strategic decisions and business activities. As such, the risk management systems can become powerful as an integral part of the management process and the setting of the organizational agenda. On the other hand, risk management systems are not necessarily seen by top management and the board as addressing key strategic concerns but is more used as a 'monitoring and alarm' approach akin to the diagnostic systems. In this case, the risk management frameworks may turn into a mere 'box-ticking' compliance exercise responding to regulatory requirements.

In conclusion, strategy scholars have for decades been conceptualizing risk, and the ability to manage the inherent exposures in strategic decision processes and the development of strategic issue management systems can be seen as a potential precursor to SRM. Originating from the field of accounting and finance, contemporary ERM frameworks provide firms with diagnostic controls where the frameworks in their current form assume a top-down driven strategy-making process and often adopt an insurance perspective to risk management. Alternatively, if ERM is used interactively with strategy-making, it may provide the possibility of integrating strategic and risk management to deal more effectively with turbulent environments by not only providing assurance but potentially shaping strategic decisions and providing support for ongoing business activities.

Notes

1 RIMS (2017) survey of 397 risk professionals across 14 different industries suggests that 29% of companies adopted the COSO framework (37% of financial firms), 25% embraced the ISO31000 standard, and 20% did not follow any particular framework in defining their "ERM" practices.
2 Beasley, Branson, and Hancock have partnered over more than ten years with the American Institute of Certified Public Accountants' (AICPA) Business, Industry, and Government Team to survey business leaders about a number of characteristics related to their current enterprise-wide risk management efforts.

4 Empirical studies and insights

Empirical research on the strategic implications of enterprise risk management (ERM) has mainly focused on three areas: the characteristics of ERM adopters, the impact of ERM on firm value and performance, and ERM applications in specific organizational settings. Despite the increasing interest in ERM, comprehensive theories on ERM do not exist and the empirical research on ERM has so far been inconclusive in systematically documenting the effects of specific ERM practices. The variation in results can be ascribed to at least two primary factors. To begin with, it has been difficult to develop a common reliable ERM construct where many studies use dichotomous variables as indicators of ERM implementation. Some studies search for the use of 'ERM' in annual reports as indicator of adherence to ERM (Quon, Zeghal and Maingot, 2012; Lundquist and Vilhelmsson, 2018). Since most firms disclose little information about their concrete ERM practices, several studies use appointment of a chief risk officer (CRO) as a proxy for ERM implementation searching for CRO hiring announcements among sampled firms from publicly available information (Liebenberg and Hoyt, 2003; Pagach and Warr, 2011). Beasley, Clune and Hermanson (2005) provide empirical support for a positive relationship between the presence of a CRO and the adoption of ERM as justification for using CRO appointments as a proxy for ERM implementation.

Nevertheless, measuring ERM with a binary variable is criticized for being inadequate as it oversimplifies things and fails to capture the nuances of ERM practices. Hence, it does not take into account to what extent the ERM framework and the implied processes are executed within an organization (Beasley, Pagach and Warr, 2008; Mikes and Kaplan, 2014). As noted by Mikes and Kaplan (2014), ERM exists in a variety of forms "deployed at different levels, for different purposes, by different staff groups in different organizations" (p. 8). The lack of a comprehensive ERM framework, or not having an official

CRO, does not necessarily indicate that basic ERM processes are absent. The firms may simply not have an articulated ERM vocabulary, or a CRO, yet they could have risk management practices embedded in their managerial actions and tactics (Corvellec, 2009). It is also possible that other executives are responsible for ERM processes than an official CRO (Liebenberg and Hoyt, 2003). Furthermore, the effect of adopting ERM programs is assessed against different indicators and measures of organizational performance. Whereas Beasley et al. (2008) use market reactions represented by changes in stock price as a measure of ERM valuation, Hoyt and Liebenberg (2011) measure firm value using Tobin's Q. Hence, the inconsistent use of measures of organizational performance complicates the generalizability of results.

Due to the limitations of binary proxies as indicators for ERM implementation, other studies have moved beyond use of dichotomous variables. For example, Gordon et al. (2009) develop an index for ERM that quantifies the quality of the ERM application based on the ability to achieve four objectives established by COSO (2004). McShane, Nair and Rustambekov (2011) and Baxter et al. (2013) use Standard & Poor's (S&P) risk management rating of insurance companies as a proxy for the level of ERM sophistication. The ERM rating is added to the eight components that S&P uses to rate the financial strength of insurers (S&P, 2012). However, Lundquist (2014) raises concern that the S&P ERM rating has not been examined for its appropriateness in ERM studies and is limited to insurance companies. Quon et al. (2012) measure ERM adoption by the level of risk assessment reported in annual reports and financial statements. Lundquist and Vilhelmsson (2018) use a comprehensive word search for ERM phrases together with other dimensions of ERM, such as risk appetite and combinations of risk, response, and plan, to develop an aggregate measure of the degree of ERM implementation. Other researchers attempt to develop their own measures derived from the COSO framework (COSO, 2004) to explore the level of ERM implementation (e.g., Beasley et al., 2005; Gates, Nicolas and Walker, 2012; Paape and Spekle, 2012; Sax and Torp, 2015; Aleisa, 2018).

Adopting ERM – the antecedents

Previous empirical studies show that adoption of ERM is associated with a number of internal factors such as having a CRO, financial leverage, firm size, profitability and turnover, international diversification, institutional ownership, business strategy, and emphasis on shareholder maximization. Other studies have also looked at links to external factors including globalization, deregulation, and industry consolidation (e.g., Lam and Kawamoto, 1997; Miccolis and Shah, 2000; Liebenberg and Hoyt, 2003).

Chief risk officer (CRO)

An increasing number of firms appoint CROs and a survey by Accenture in 2013[1] finds that 96% of the responding large firms had a CRO in 2013 and that the presence of a CRO (or equivalent senior risk executive) increased from 78% in 2011. The increasing emphasis on a CRO is presumed to fulfill the following formal tasks (Lam, 2003; Taylor, 2014):

- Establish an integrated risk management framework for all aspects of risk across the entire organization.
- Develop the risk management policies including the quantification and allocation of risk appetite by establishing specific risk limits/tolerance levels.
- Communicate goals and objectives for the group risk policy and framework.
- Manage the implementation, maintenance, and continuous improvement of the group risk policy and framework.
- Manage the information system supporting the risk policy and framework.
- Deliver metrics and risk reports to the executive management, the board, risk/audit committee, and risk advisory group to support risk-based decision-making.
- Review the risk profiles throughout the organization and propose proper levels of capital to risk exposures.
- Create a risk-aware and risk-conscious culture through communication and training, risk-based performance measures, incentive systems, and change management programs.

In addition, the practitioner literature on risk management suggests that CROs should be proactive communicators of risk with themselves in a "strategic business advisor" capacity (KPMG, 2011, p. 27) rather than being reactive control agents. Mikes (2014) suggests that the role of the CRO is less about packaging and marketing the risk management idea but more to facilitate a specific risk language as legitimate business jargon in the organization. By acting as facilitator of risk discussions rather than bringing formal authority, the CRO can use the principles of risk management in the business as opposed to establishing a control function. The CRO role is about building informal network relationships among executives and business managers by carefully balancing the CRO position between a compliance champion and a business partner, keeping distance yet staying involved. To demonstrate commitment to ERM, many firms choose to appoint a CRO and locate the responsibility for the risk management processes at a senior executive (Paapa and Spekle, 2011) by speeding up the ERM implementation through top management support (Beasley et al., 2008). Hence, the presence of a CRO is found to have a significant impact on the implementation of ERM (Beasley et al., 2005), where the CRO encourages the firm to engage in ERM practices (Lam and Kawamoto, 1997). This is supported by Kleffner, Lee and McGannon (2003) who find that the presence of a CRO influences eventual ERM implementation. Beasley et al. (2005) identify the degree to which firms have implemented ERM based on survey data. Their study shows that the existence of a CRO constitutes a significant determinant for the application of ERM.

Financial leverage

Financial leverage is an indicator of the capital structure and is proportional to the amount of borrowing adopted by the firm typically measured by the ratio of total debt to total assets (e.g., Keown, Martin and Petty, 2008). The empirical findings on the effect of financial leverage on ERM adoption are ambiguous. Liebenberg and Hoyt (2003), Pagach and Warr (2011), and Golshan and Rasid (2012) find that financial leverage is positively related to ERM implementation. However, in later studies, Hoyt and Liebenberg (2011) find significant negative relationships. Financial leverage can be a useful way to fund projects for the future growth of the firm, but higher leverage (and debts) also increase the likelihood of (and possible costs from) financial distress and eventual bankruptcy. This argues that leveraged firms adopt ERM programs to reduce the likelihood of financial distress (Pagach and Warr, 2011). In contrast, Hoyt and Liebenberg's (2011) studies suggest that companies with lower financial leverage, and thus lower financial risk, may decide in favor of an ERM system to be able to take on more risk.

Financial slack

Financial slack reflects a cushion, or buffer, the firm establishes to deal with periods of pressure on the operating cash flows. It can be measured by the amount of liquid assets (such as cash or marketable securities) a firm has at hand to continue operations making up for any deficits in operating cash flows (Pagach and Warr, 2011). While firms may increase financial slack to reduce the probability of financial distress, it is also reasonable that firms may reduce the level of financial slack if the risk management practices are effective (Pagach and Warr, 2011). In a study of the insurance sector, Bohnert et al. (2019) find that insurance companies with 'high-quality' ERM programs tend to have more financial slack than insurers with lower quality ERM programs. On the other hand, Hoyt and Liebenberg (2011) find a negative relationship between financial slack and ERM adoption and note that ERM users may be able to reduce the level of financial slack because of improved risk management capabilities.

Firm size

Larger company size is generally associated with increasing scope and complexity of risks, which increases the likelihood of ERM implementation (Paape and Spekle, 2012). Adopting ERM is a rather significant decision and a major resource commitment that signals an organizational change initiative. McShane, Nair and Rustambekov (2011) argue that the required financial and human resources, including IT systems, is an obstacle for firms that want to adopt ERM programs, where larger organizations have more resources to implement ERM. Beasley et al. (2005) found that company size is a significant factor for ERM adoption, which is confirmed in subsequent studies by Hoyt and Liebenberg (2011) and Pagach and Warr (2011). A larger organization increases the scope and complexity of risks that require a formal risk management system as well as they have more resources available to implement ERM.

Ownership structure

Pagach and Warr (2011) suggest that firms with greater institutional ownership are under greater pressure to adopt an ERM program. Liebenberg and Hoyt (2003) argue that pressure from major shareholders is an important force driving adoption of ERM (cf. also Mikes, 2009). Desender and Lafuente (2011) further argue that firms with concentrated ownership, with at least one large shareholder, are more likely to adopt ERM. As large investors have a greater stake in the organization, they have an interest in imposing risk-adjusted decision-making practices to enhance firm value as ERM advocates. Firms with a higher share of institutional ownership are assumed to be under higher pressure to introduce a control system than those with more dispersed ownership, and thus are more inclined to implement an ERM framework (Liebenberg and Hoyt, 2003; Hoyt and Liebenberg, 2011). Pagach and Warr (2011) similarly find that firms with higher institutional ownership are more likely to adopt ERM. Bohnert et al. (2019) observe that institutional shareholders indeed appear to apply pressure to develop a holistic corporate risk management system.

Earnings and stock price volatility

One of the benefits of ERM is argued to be lower volatility in earnings, cash flows, and stock price, where smoothing of performance outcomes reduces the likelihood of extreme lower tail outcomes (Gatzert and Martin, 2015). Empirical studies typically express volatility as the coefficient of variation in earnings before interest and taxes, operating cash flows, or stock price measured as the annualized standard deviation (Pagach and Warr, 2011). Hence, firms with more erratic earnings, cash flows, or stock prices would benefit more from ERM due to the ability to smoothen earnings flows and better control stock price reactions. Pagach and Warr (2011) find that firms with more volatile earnings and poor stock market performance are more likely to initiate an ERM program. Likewise, Bohnert et al. (2019) show that volatility of earnings and stock prices are significant predictors of an ERM program.

Diversification

By spreading operations across industries and geographies, firms are less vulnerable to changes in the business context or local market conditions (Reuer and Leiblein, 2000; Andersen, 2011). Lam (2003) defines diversification as the ability to lower the total exposure of the enterprise by spreading activities across many distinct projects, where the total risk from a collection of diverse risk is less than the sum of those isolated risks. Diversification may reduce the overall economic and political risks from operating in a single country or in a single business. A higher diversification of company activities should also increase the complexity of the aggregated risks, which is an incentive for adopting an ERM program. Thus, it is argued that there is a positive relationship between level of diversification and ERM adoption (Golshan and Rasid, 2012). The empirical results do not confirm significant relationships between diversification and ERM adoption (Hoyt and Liebenberg, 2011; Pagach and Warr, 2011; Golshan and Rasid, 2012). Liebenberg and Hoyt (2003) test whether US companies are more likely to adopt ERM when they have subsidiaries in the UK or Canada, but do not find empirical support for this. Conversely, Hoyt and Liebenberg (2011) find a negative relationship between international diversification and ERM in the insurance industry.

Business strategy

One of the internal factors that could influence ERM adoption is business strategy, as ERM design and implementation supposedly is generated by the chosen strategy and related objectives. Soltanizadeh et al. (2016) find that companies pursuing a strategy of 'cost leadership' are more likely to implement ERM compared to those pursuing a 'differentiation' strategy. However, studies on the relationship between firm strategy and ERM adoption remain scarce.

Industry and location

Regulators in different countries and industries play an important role in the adoption of ERM programs as legal requirements push firms to document adherence to formal risk management practices (Kleffner et al., 2003; Collier, Berry and Burke, 2006). Examples of such regulatory pressure include the Guidelines on Corporate Governance Principles for Banks by the Basel Committee on Banking Supervision, the NYSE Corporate Governance Rules and the Sarbanes-Oxley Act in the USA, and the Combined Code on Corporate Governance in the UK and the Netherlands. While these codes apply to publicly listed firms, the governance rules also set standards among private, (semi-) public, and not-for-profit organizations. These codes call for some form of systematic risk management practices, creating expectations that the organizations adopt an ERM program (cf. Collier, Berry and Burke, 2006). The financial and energy sectors are considered more prone to implement ERM systems compared to other industries (Golshan and Rasid, 2012). Liebenberg and Hoyt (2003) and Pagach and Warr (2011) confirm that organizations in financial services are more likely to be ERM adopters. A recent survey by RIMS (2017) reports that 92% of financial institutions have full, or partially integrated, ERM programs. Liebenberg and Hoyt (2003) argue that internationally diversified firms operating in countries with more stringently regulated corporate governance and risk management control approaches, such as the UK and Canada, are more likely to adopt an ERM program. Similarly, Beasley et al. (2005) observe that US organizations have less developed ERM systems compared to other countries where ERM frameworks have been in place for a longer time. Hence, Golshan and Rasid (2012) hypothesize that firms headquartered in or with subsidiaries in the UK, Canada, Australia, and New Zealand are more likely to implement ERM frameworks, but fail to find support for this claim. The impact of industry is also studied by Beasley et al. (2005) who find that the banking, education, and insurance industries are more prone to develop ERM systems.

ERM and performance

There is an increasing trend among firms to adopt ERM as a leading approach to deal with all organizational exposures, including strategic risks, even though there is an ongoing debate on the tangible and intangible benefits to be derived from ERM implementation. ERM drives value creation not only in terms of efficiency and downside loss avoidance but also through enhanced decision-making capabilities and increased risk awareness (Bromiley et al., 2014). In a survey of 150 audit and risk management executives, Gates et al. (2012) find that the use of ERM leads to increased management consensus, better-informed decisions, enhanced risk-taking communication, and management accountability. By identifying risks with upside potential, firms can arguably achieve a competitive advantage from ERM (Beasley et al., 2015). This advantage should lower a firm's overall risk of failure and increase the upside gains in firm performance and value. The reported benefits from effective ERM implementation include:

- Enhancing firm performance
- Reducing the cost of capital
- Increasing capital efficiency
- Decreasing earnings and stock price volatility
- Increasing firm value

Firm performance

By identifying and reacting to risks related to objectives, management can gain better oversight and make better decision, which translates into increased ability to meet strategic goals and increase profitability (Gates et al., 2012). Grace et al. (2014) measure firm performance as the ability to marshal firm resources to gain cost efficiencies and increase return on assets (ROA). Their study finds that US insurance companies emphasizing ERM-related activities (e.g., CRO, dedicated risk committees, a risk management function, risk management reporting to the board) achieve higher cost efficiency and ROA (Grace et al., 2014). They also find that moving from simple risk-based capital allocation models to more advanced models – using scenarios, stress testing, and stochastic simulations – fails to add further performance improvements. Eckles, Hoyt and Miller (2014a) find that ERM adopting firms experience increasing operating profits per unit of risk. In a study of ERM in nonfinancial firms, Callahan and Soileau (2017) find that firms with higher ERM process maturity have better operating performance than their industry peers measured by industry-adjusted ROA and return on equity (ROE) ratios. Baxter et al. (2013) use S&P's ERM rating as a proxy for ERM implementation and find a significant positive relationship between ERM and operating performance among insurance companies and banks. In another study, Nair et al. (2014) find that firms with high S&P ERM ratings are associated with superior profitability measured by ROA during the post-crisis upturn.

Nevertheless, not all studies have found a positive relationship between ERM adoption and firm performance. Quon et al. (2012) studied ERM among nonfinancial companies listed on the Toronto Stock Exchange through analyses of annual reports. They examined the effect of ERM implementation on firm performance measured by a variety of market-based, operational, and accounting performance measures, including sales growth, EBIT margins, and Tobin's Q, but still failed to find any relationship to performance.

Cost of capital

ERM adoption can arguably be used by firms to reduce the cost of capital and provide the firm with better access to the capital markets as improved disclosure of firm exposures reduces information asymmetries, which enhances investor confidence (Miccolis and Shah, 2000; Liebenberg and Hoyt, 2003; Nocco and Stulz, 2006; Pagach and Warr, 2011). It is further argued that ERM can improve the credit rating (S&P, 2012) and thereby reduce the cost of external financing. In a study of US insurance companies, Berry-Stölzle and Xu (2018) find that ERM is associated with lower cost of capital.

Capital efficiency

Managing risks in a holistic way should provide a better understanding of the aggregated corporate exposures contributed by different business units. Similarly, Lam (2014) argues that ERM can improve ROE and enhance shareholder value by allocating capital to the business units that promise the highest risk-adjusted return. Accordingly, ERM should provide a more objective basis for allocating resources among alternative investment opportunities, resulting in improved capital efficiency and higher ROE (Meulbroek, 2002). Integrating all risk classes across units should help the company avoid duplication of risk management efforts while exploiting natural hedges (Hoyt and Liebenberg, 2011).

Corporate earnings

Based on arguments from value maximization theory, some scholars argue that ERM can reduce earnings and stock price volatility and thereby enhance shareholder value (Krause and Tse, 2016). Stulz (1996) argues that a potential value-creating role of ERM is to reduce the effect of costly lower tail outcomes. Lower tail outcomes represent negative earnings following extreme financial events that increase the probability of financial distress. The total risk management process can smooth earnings and cash flows, thereby reducing volatility and the chance of extreme events. In one study, Nair et al. (2014) find that ERM has significant associations to profitability as well as stock price. They find that a high S&P ERM rating is associated with a smaller decline in stock price during a downturn indicated by percentage drop in stock price from a pre-crisis high to the lowest point during the crisis (Nair et al., 2014). Similarly, Eckles, Hoyt and Miller (2014b) find that firms adopting ERM reduce the volatility of stock returns and become stronger over time.

Share price and firm value

ERM proponents argue that it can enhance shareholder value and maximize wealth as the ultimate corporate risk management goal (Nocco and Stulz, 2006). However, the empirical findings on the relationship between ERM implementation and firm value have been very inconsistent. In their study of insurance companies, Hoyt and Liebenberg (2011) found that firms with ERM initiatives are associated with larger value premiums. McShane et al. (2011) also studied insurance companies and demonstrate that firms emphasizing control systems to manage risks increase firm value. Yet, they do not find a significant relationship between firm value and moving beyond silo risk management toward coordinated ERM efforts. Baxter et al. (2013) examine the association between ERM implementation and firm value in a sample of 165 banks and insurance companies and conclude that ERM does not lead to higher firm value. Beasley et al.'s (2008) study 120 US firms to investigate how stock markets react to news of hiring a CRO. They find that in the nonfinancial sectors, markets react positively to ERM adoption among large firms with high earnings volatility. In contrast, Lin, Wen and Yu (2012) find a strong negative relationship between adoption of an ERM program and firm value.

Financial leverage

Adherence to ERM is said to add value by enhancing much of the upside potential while reducing the probability of financial distress and downside loss (Pagach and Warr, 2011). Firms can become more risk aware when they adopt ERM and reduce financial leverage (Hoyt and Liebenberg, 2011) to reduce financial risk (Miller and Bromiley, 1990) and financial distress (Leland and Pyle, 1977; Al-Najjar and Taylor, 2008). By maintaining lower leverage ratios, firms retain more capital reserves as a buffer to fund promising business propositions including R&D investments and new product launches (O'Brien, 2003), which can support valuable investment projects (Andersen, 2009). Firms may also decide to increase leverage due to improved risk management capabilities (Hoyt and Liebenberg, 2011). There is still limited empirical research exploring this relationship, but Sax and Andersen (2018) find a significant negative association between ERM and financial leverage.

Contingency factors

Some studies refer to contingency theory to explain how specific contextual factors may be associated with ERM implementation (Mikes and Kaplan, 2014), where the performance of ERM programs is a function of the match with those factors (Gordon et al., 2009). Hence, Rochette (2009) emphasizes a strong risk culture and adequate incentive system as prerequisites for successful implementation of ERM programs. Sax and Torp (2015) argue that ERM success is contingent upon a risk management culture that encourages people to raise their voice and report on risk where they are not penalized or blamed but rather are rewarded for such behavior. Management should support internal knowledge transfer and learning processes and embrace initiatives for employee involvement, which should increase the likelihood of successful ERM programs. Research shows that positive performance effects of ERM depend on a participative leadership style, which is contingent on a corporate culture where employees feel safe to speak up (Sax and Torp, 2015). Beasley et al. (2015) find that the perception of ERM as an important strategic tool is stronger in firms with a risk committee that provide executives with formal risk management training and update their key risks. Studying one-year excess stock market returns in a sample of 112 US firms, Gordon et al. (2009) find that positive relationships between ERM and firm value are contingent on the level of environmental uncertainty, the degree of competition, firm size, organizational complexity, and board monitoring. Beasley et al. (2005) also find that top management support is key for effective ERM implementation. In a study of the interplay between ERM, strategic planning, and performance among 260 large Danish companies, Sax and Andersen (2018) find that strategic planning mediates the positive effect of ERM on performance (measured as ROA). They argue that ERM increases risk awareness and treatment, which, in turn, enhance the ability to coordinate risk initiatives across business plans in the strategic planning process as a rational way to program organizational actions. Consequently, organizations should emphasize strategic planning as a way to enhance the value of ERM.

In summary, many studies provide strong theoretical arguments for potential value to be gained from implementation of ERM as a total risk management approach that also considers operational and strategic exposures. However, the empirical evidence regarding the claimed benefits is rather inconclusive. Hence, the empirical studies have so far provided little evidence on the value-creating effect from ERM adoption despite strong theoretical arguments and institutional motivations.

ERM versus strategic management

The ERM process has been described as a systematic and iterative process of objective setting, risk identification, analysis and evaluation, risk treatment, reporting, and monitoring (Moeller, 2007). Integrating a portfolio of corporate risks requires the recognition of major risk factors where associated events are evaluated and the resulting exposures reported (Schiller and Pripch, 2014). Strategic management scholars have similarly argued that the process of identifying, analyzing, and dealing with risks and opportunities is key for the ability to manage strategic risks (Baird and Thomas, 1985) and firm adoption (Milliken, 1990). Kiesler and Sproull (1982, p. 548) argue that "sensing, the cognitive processes of noticing and constructing meaning about environmental change" is an essential component of managing in rapidly changing contexts as a prerequisite for taking responsive actions. The ERM approach presumes that major risks can be identified in advance, that they can be assessed (and managed) unambiguously, and that the associated exposures can be reported without friction to the top of the organization. These assumptions are consistent with the rational decision-making model that underpins the strategic management process premised on the assumption that decision-makers have complete information to maximize decision outputs. The rational decision-making model investigates multiple alternatives, analyses the costs and benefits of alternatives, makes detailed plans for implementation, and integrates the decisions into an overarching strategy (e.g., Miller and Friesen, 1983; Eisenhardt, 1989). Hitt and Tyler (1991) describe rational strategic decision-making as "a series of ... analytical processes whereby objective criteria are used to evaluate strategic alternatives" (p. 329). It is argued that the orientation toward organizational goals makes it more likely that rational decision-making will be effective (Dean and Sharfman, 1996).

Since the (official) purpose of ERM is to assure fulfillment of strategic objectives (COSO, 2004), a natural first step is to make sure that proper objectives are in place before management can identify events that might affect their achievement. Hence, most ERM frameworks assume that risks should be identified based on the company's objectives. COSO (2017) further emphasizes that the objectives should be aligned with the risk appetite and tolerance level determined by top management and the board. Gates et al. (2012) find a positive association between objective setting and risk identification and argue that risks from a company-wide perspective within clearly defined risk tolerances makes it easier to create a risk inventory for the business with tools to evaluate and monitor the risks (Gates et al. 2012). While the purpose of ERM is not to determine the objectives and strategy per se, it is seen as support for 'strategy setting' where appetite for risk is set in advance as a basis for choosing between alternative strategies supporting operational and strategic decisions (COSO, 2017). The ERM framework can arguably determine the criteria to assess how a given strategy may affect the risk profile of the firm and how sensitive the aggregated exposure it is to changes in underlying assumptions and unexpected changes with respect to achieving the stated objectives (ibid).

Parts of the management literature have defined decisions as a specific commitment to action that typically involves a commitment of resources (e.g., Mintzberg et al., 1976). As Ocasio points out, decisions "may or may not be implemented and lead to strategic change" (1997, p. 201). Consequently, a decision process is a set of actions that start with identification of a stimulus for action, development of alternative solutions, and ends with the selection of a specific solution

Figure 4.1 Strategic risk management process framework.

and a commitment to action (Mintzberg et al., 1976). Similarly, Daft and Weick (1984) outline three phases of organizational interpretation: scanning, interpretation, and learning. Dutton and Ottensmeyer (1987) present similar phases of perceiving, analyzing, and responding to major strategic issues much like strategic sense-making comprised by perceiving, analyzing, and responding. Although the stimulus for action (i.e., the issue or risk event) and the phases from risk identification to action have been labeled differently across studies, the connotation is essentially the same. Other studies include an additional element of 'issue-selling' where much effort is devoted to bring relevant risk issue(s) to the attention of senior decision-makers (Dutton and Duncan, 1987a; Dutton et al., 1997).

The process of risk identification, analysis and evaluation, selling, and response are all elements of conventional strategic (planning) and risk management processes (Figure 4.1). The feedback loops represent the cyclical nature of the process and emphasize that current actions and experiences gained from them influence subsequent risk identification and handling. Hence, feedback from risk treatment may provide new insights about emergent risks that influence ongoing risk identification and assessment activities.

Risk identification

The purpose of risk identification is to recognize and describe events that may prevent an organization from achieving its objectives (ISO 31000, 2018). The organization must first identify the potential risk factors to establish an inventory of risks constituted by a formal listing of the risks faced by the entity (COSO, 2017). This first step in the ERM process implies the formalized nature of the process as it implicitly assumes that all risks can be recognized in advance. COSO (2017) acknowledges that some risks will remain unknown and for which there are "no reasonable expectations that the organization would consider during risk identification." However, the framework does not provide guidance on how firms should deal with these unknown risks. Similarly, the identification of risks and opportunities (often referred to as threats and opportunities in strategy) typically constitutes the first phase of the analytical strategic management process (Wheelen and Hunger, 2010). The identification of strategic risks has received different descriptions in the literature, such as awareness (Lant, Milliken and Batra, 1992), strategic surveillance (Schreyogg and Steinmann, 1987; Preble, 1992), and environmental scanning (Aguilar, 1967). Firms that acquire extensive information before making decisions are better equipped to identify viable choices (Dean and Sharfman, 1996).

Aguilar (1967) defines environmental scanning as acquisition of information "about events and relationships in a company's outside environment, the knowledge of which would assist top management in its task of charting the company's future course of action" (p. 1). He distinguishes between four modes of scanning: undirected viewing, conditioned viewing, informal search, and formal search (Aguilar, 1967). ERM can provide firms with a formal search mode since the risk identification phase in ERM is conceived as a deliberate effort followed by an active search to obtain more specific information related to the identified risks. ERM does not really consider other environmental scanning modes. Environmental scanning depends on both individual and organizational risk perception as this influences what is observed. At the individual level, "perceptual selection determines to which issues in the environment top-level decision-makers will devote their scarce cognitive processing capacities" (Heugens, 2001). At the firm level, various characteristics of the strategic planning process determine the array of risks the organization takes into account when making decisions (Dutton and Duncan, 1987b). However, despite the potential to influence strategic planning, Fahey and King (1977) argue that environmental scanning has been poorly integrated into strategic planning. They divide scanning into irregular, regular, and continuous modes. The ERM frameworks emphasize the regular and continuous scanning modes, where organizations have systematic and periodic risk identification combined with continuous monitoring and review cycles. The continuous approach is structured with clear responsibilities for risk identification, established channels for information, and explicit linkages between risk identification and planning. It supports the "variety of choices inherent in strategic planning" (Fahey and King, 1977, p. 63) as opposed to the specific choices in the regular risk identification mode. Hence, the ERM approach can be seen as a mechanism that considers both of these modes supporting the choice among alternative strategies and assessing potential risks that arise from the chosen strategy, but with little consideration for irregular scanning.

In the management literature, risk identification has been described as an organizational necessity for long-term survival (Weitzel and Jonsson, 1989). Failure to scan external and internal environments and identify related risks is early indicator of firm deterioration (Daft and Weick, 1984; Thomas and McDaniel, 1990; Thomas, Clark and Gioia, 1993). Hence, Daft, Sormunen and Parks (1988) find a positive relationship between firm profitability and environmental scanning. Garg, Walters and Priem (2003) argue that both internal and external scanning are important in line with the subset of ERM that focuses on operational risk and not only external factors. Hambrick (1982) provides an empirical account of the relationship between external environmental scanning by executives and the organization's strategy and finds that executives do not use scanning to reinforce their strategies. Scanning by itself is not a basis for competitive advantage, but success follows from the ability to act upon environmental information. Hence, scanning is an important initial step in a chain of activities that leads to organizational adaption since an "organization's executives can only act on those phenomena to which their attention is drawn" (Hambrick, 1981, p. 299).

Risk analysis and evaluation

After identifying risks, they are analyzed and evaluated to create a deeper understanding of the changing environment (Paine and Anderson, 1977) where "the imposition of meaning on issues characterized by ambiguity has become a hallmark of the modern top management" (Thomas et al., 1993, p. 240). The risk assessment is important to prioritize different risk factors according to potential severity (impact and likelihood) and importance in view of business objectives and risk appetite. This helps management inform strategic decisions and evaluate allocations to mitigate different risks (COSO, 2017). Risk analysis and evaluation, referred inter alia to as interpretation, or diagnosis in the strategy literature, is where management seeks to understand the evoked stimuli and determine cause-effect relationships (Mintzberg et al., 1976). As Barr explains, "a key component in a firm's strategic response to unfamiliar environmental events is the interpretation managers develop about the event itself" (1998, p. 644). Following Daft and Weick's (1984) definition of interpretation, the risk analysis and evaluation phase is where managers translate the risks and bring meaning to the data before taking action (Daft and Weick, 1984).

Mintzberg et al. (1976) stress that "diagnosis is probably the single most important routine, since it determines ... the subsequent course of action" (p. 274). The phase of interpretation has been seen as critical to the strategic management process because a deeper understanding of the environmental context is imperative to firm success and survival (Dutton and Duncan, 1987a). In other words, the way managers diagnose risks can be critical since variations in diagnosis can lead to vastly different strategic responses (Dutton and Duncan, 1987b; Dutton and Dukerich, 1991; Lant, Milliken and Batra, 1992).

However, interpretation of risks is not a straightforward process as "strategic issues do not activate decision-makers' attention in packaged form" (Dutton and Duncan, 1987a, p. 280). Different ways of diagnosing may result in more or less effective strategic decisions with varied levels of performance outcomes (Meyer, 1982; Gooding and Kinicki, 1995). ERM and the rational decision-making model advocate formal analysis as support for strategic decisions. In a study of formal analysis in strategic decision-making, Langley (1990) found that the purpose of formal analysis is twofold. First, the analysis is used as input to decisions to control implementation and ensure that actions are taken. Second, the analysis is used as a political tool to persuade in internal negotiations about what actions should be taken. Similarly, Langley (1990) and Mueller, Mone and Barker (2007) investigate the effects of formal analysis as information, persuasion, communication, control, direction, and symbolism. They found instrumental use of information in decision processes positively linked to organizational performance in both high and low dynamism environments (Mueller et al., 2007). In dynamic environments, analyses for symbolic control purposes were positively associated with performance whereas analysis for persuasion resulted in lower performance.

Risk 'selling'

Once the risks have been identified and evaluated, the risk manager in the organization communicates with other organizational members, including senior management, to gain buy-in and invite proper responses (Brown and Eisenhart, 1997). This is the process of 'selling' the risk (a notion borrowed from Dutton and Ashford's, 1993 issue-selling concept) and is the part where senior management's attention is directed toward the risks that might warrant adjustments to the organization's strategic direction. For Dutton and Ashford (1993), the 'selling' of risks (or strategic issues) is central in explaining how and where senior management allocates time and attention.

According to Heugens (2001), this part "determines to which issues in their environment top-level decision-makers will devote their scarce cognitive processing capabilities." Detert and Burris (2007) argue that "even the most proactive or satisfied employees are likely to 'read the wind' as to whether it is safe and/or worthwhile to speak up in their particular context" (p. 869). Accordingly, Dutton and Ashford (1993) see issue-selling as important to individuals and the organization. Issue-selling facilitates the establishment of a strategic agenda and course of action by prompting the attention of top management. Issues that are sold successfully by a collective group of employees to top management make them feel part of the corporate identity. For individuals, issues are "part of the currency through which their careers are made or broken" (Dutton and Ashford, 1993, p. 402) that may result in promotion and satisfaction, whereas potential downsides can lead to demotion or humiliation (Detert and Burris, 2007). In view of these impediments, several firms have implemented whistleblowing programs and anonymous risk voting systems to ensure participation and honesty (Fraser and Simkins, 2009).

COSO (2017) suggests the use of tools like 'heat maps' to assess results from risk analysis and highlight the relative severity of various risks to the achievement of strategic objectives. Jordan, Jørgensen and Mitterhofer (2013) investigate the use of heat maps to communicate risks and find that appearance on a heat map makes it more likely to receive attention and be considered. They show that tool-based communication is important to obtain attention among decision-makers and among risk managers as a way to 'translate' risk insights to formats that management can turn into action (Jordan et al., 2013). Braumann (2018) further argues that this is why risk awareness and assessment is crucial for effective risk management.

The strategic issue-selling literature stresses that organizational context is important to initiate the issue-selling process. Dutton et al. (1997) find that employees consider whether it is 'safe' to voice concerns and bring attention to critical issues. Similarly, Floyd and Wooldridge (1997) argue that contexts where employees feel it is safe to speak up about critical issues and potential problems are a key element for organizational adaptability. The feeling of psychological safety is a precursor for speaking up as employees assess potential rewards and punishments that issue-selling might impose on them (Ashford et al., 1998). Accordingly, Sax and Torp (2015) investigate the role of leadership style find that firms with a top management that invites input from employees in decision-making are more successful in adopting ERM practices. They also find that a work environment where lower level managers feel safe raising concerns is a precursor for participative leadership (Sax and Torp, 2015). Similarly, Mikes and Kaplan (2014) find that management support in a 'no-blame' culture encourages people to speak up on potential risk issues, which is important for successful ERM adoption.

Risk treatment

The treatment of risk has been conceived as a process that generates strategic action based on an interpretation or assessment of the exposures in the given environmental context (Daft and Weick, 1984). It constitutes the stage in a strategic decision where "the level of effort and commitment that top-level decision-makers are willing to devote to action designed to resolve an issue" is determined (Daft and Weick, 1984, p. 286). The associated analysis and evaluation of risks enables the organization to make informed choices by accepting, avoiding, mitigating, or transferring underlying exposures (Lam, 2003; Moeller, 2007). For all the identified risks, management should deploy risk-treating actions considering the severity of impact prioritizing the risks in view of the business context and strategic objectives (COSO, 2017). The formal risk responses comprise the following:

- *Accept exposure* – when the risk is within risk appetite, or when the costs of taking action outweigh the potential downsides, the organization can choose not to take action to change the severity of the risk.
- *Avoid exposure* – if it is impossible to identify a response that reduces the risk to an acceptable level of severity, the organization can choose to remove the risk, for example, by terminating a product line or withdrawing from a specific market.
- *Control/mitigate/reduce exposure* – where the identified risk is outside the risk appetite, the organization can decide to reduce the severity of the risk by limiting the impact or the likelihood of the event, for example, by reducing sale targets or reducing errors by investing in automaton, and so on.
- *Transfer/share exposure* – when the risk exceeds the risk appetite, an alternative response can be to reduce the severity of the risk by transferring the risk, for example, by outsourcing exposed activities to specialist service providers, purchasing insurance covers, or engaging in hedging transactions.
- *Increase/exploit exposure/opportunities* – where the risk is considered not only to be within the risk appetite but substantially below

the threshold, the organization can consider increasing the exposure, for example, by expanding into new markets, developing new products, and so on.

Some of these risk responses may lead to a revision of the official strategy to align business objectives with the stated risk appetite (COSO, 2017). Hence, the ERM approach differs from traditional risk management by the possibility to consider the upside potential of identified risks. In comparison, strategic planning has been referred to as "the continuous process of making present entrepreneurial (risk-taking) decisions systematically" by "organizing systematically the efforts needed to carry out these decisions" (Drucker, 1974, p. 125). That is, this (potential) aspect of the ERM framework links to the function of a strategic planning process, which makes some researchers argue that ERM should be an integral part of strategic planning and decision-making throughout the organization (e.g., Beasley and Frigo, 2010; Braumann, 2018; Sax and Andersen, 2018). Integrating risk management practices with strategic planning can provide management with essential risk information as support for decisions to choose among alternative strategies. Liedtka (2000) has suggested that integrating ERM with strategic planning can generate a portfolio view of all risks and assess proper risk treatment strategies where strategic planning coordinates corporate actions. Risk management may also assess whether strategic initiatives generate excessive exposures (Beasley and Frigo, 2010). Hence, there seems to be meaningful ways in which risk management practices can be linked to strategic planning in ongoing execution of strategic initiatives.

Linking risk management to strategic planning

The integration of risk management with strategic planning refers to the consideration of relevant risk information in rational strategy analyses and ongoing decision-making (Braumann, 2018). Strategic planning is generally conceived as a sequence of logical steps, including development of mission, setting long-term objectives, conducting environmental analyses, pointing to a preferred strategic direction, planning needed actions, and monitoring outcomes in view of stated objectives (e.g., Andrews, 1987; Cohen and Cyert, 1973; Ansoff, 1988; Boyd and Reuning-Elliott, 1998). Strategic planning coordinates the business activities of organizational subunits within the overarching corporate mission as a way to integrate strategic actions and outline a common 'road map' for organizational initiatives (c.g., Andersen, 2004). Proponents of strategic planning claim that it can support timely and effective reaction through coordinated actions across organizational units (Andrews, 1987; Schendel and Hofer, 1979; Ansoff, 1988; Grant, 2003).

By providing direction and scope for the organization, managerial decision-makers can configure and deploy resources more effectively (Johnson, Scholes and Whittington, 2006). Strategic planning can also provide a unified sense of direction and coherence of managerial effort establishing a shared understanding among managers regarding objectives, priorities, and the means to employ for common ends (Camillus, 1975; Grant, 2003; Wolf and Floyd, 2013). A shared understanding of the corporate strategy is often considered a critical element for successful strategy implementation (Dess, 1987). A few studies have attempted to investigate the value of integrating risk management with strategic planning. Hence, Ittner and Keusch (2016) explore the influence of risk management on planning and control systems and do not find that emphasis on sophisticated risk assessments leads to changes in strategic plans. Instead, greater consideration of risks in the strategic planning process together with a greater focus on the upside potential of risk-taking seem to drive strategic change (Ittner and Keusch, 2016).

Sax and Andersen (2018) argue that ERM can serve as a valuable precursor to strategic planning and identify strategic planning as an important mediator between ERM practices and firm performance. Hence, the integration of risk management with strategic planning can advance 'strategic thinking' about where to place strategic bets and take firm-specific risks (Sax and Andersen, 2018). Braumann (2018) suggests that ERM effectiveness derives from integrating strategic planning with decision-making and finds that increased risk awareness from risk management has an indirect positive effect, providing important risk information to the strategic planning process. Hence, risk awareness is a prerequisite for integration of risk information into strategy analyses, which can enhance value indirectly by reducing the uncertainty around strategic decisions. Similarly, O'Regan et al. (2008) find that awareness of environmental threats generates more emphasis on strategic planning considerations, where planning is an important mediating mechanism between risk awareness and performance.

In conclusion, there is an increasing empirical literature determining important antecedents of ERM adoption as well as proposed benefits from ERM, but although this research stream has provided interesting insights, it remains inconclusive on essential issues. The antecedent studies seem to indicate that adherence to ERM is driven by firm size, performance volatility, management support, and industry context, suggesting that considerations about ERM implementation often are motivated by external pressures as opposed to a conscious choice. Hence, the experience of sudden life-threatening events or near-death experiences, industry-specific regulation and reporting requirements, signaling of control and resource richness, and so on are common factors that precede ERM implementation. All the while, the empirical studies on the performance effects of ERM adherence are largely inconclusive, although there are good arguments and some evidence to suggest that it can generate value if the ERM practices are integrated with strategic planning.

Note

1 The survey uses a sample of 446 large, diverse organizations, including financial services (46%) and other organizations from the utilities, health care, life sciences, and government sectors.

5   Current and emerging themes

Some key issues emerge from recent studies and research streams linked to the important influences of human factors, including behavioral, psychological, and ethical dimensions in social systems – like organizations – where the more spectacular risk events often appear at the governance rather than operational levels. Higher uncertainty associated with dynamic complex business environments constitutes another challenge as it forms a strategic risk landscape of unpredictable conditions with abrupt and potentially extreme outcomes that exceed the response capacity of conventional approaches. Hence, the potential challenges to formal ERM frameworks of dealing with the hard to foresee and quantify strategic exposures are becoming increasingly acute. This highlights a need to develop more effective strategic response capabilities where ERM practices might be integrated with dynamic organizational strategy-making, thereby opening for a promising field of research that delves into the interaction between ERM and strategic risk management (SRM) processes.

Responsiveness and ethics

Major corporate events and incidents over the past decade(s) not least the aftermath of the 2008 financial crisis provided a backdrop to reconsider the effectiveness of current approaches to manage strategic risks and think about alternative ways of dealing with major business and societal challenges. A clear revelation right after the shock imposed on the global economy was that the crisis emerged not so much due to technical failures, or operational breakdowns, but rather was associated with adverse behaviors founded in social norms, or organizational culture, and ethical shortcomings among decision-makers (RiskMinds, 2009). Hence, the common insight was that despite having 'proper' risk governance and control mechanisms in place, the way they are executed inside organizations depend on the specific climate that surrounds the agents that partake in them. One implication of this was that "risk culture and ethics need to be at the top of the agenda both of boards and regulators" (RiskMinds, 2009, p. 3).

This prompted a focus on the 'soundness' of the corporate, or organizational culture, where particularly banking regulators tried to emphasize the need to conduct business in a legal and ethical manner, but beyond that also promote more risk aware cultures among financial intermediaries in the economy. Hence, there is a need to better understand how boards, at the highest governance levels of the organization, can reinforce ethical behaviors by setting the 'tone at the top' as a way to promote risk awareness and create a strong 'risk culture' throughout the organization (BIS, 2015). Accordingly, the BIS (2015, p. 9) argues that a "fundamental component of good governance is a corporate culture and ethical behavior" and that those behavioral norms are critical to the way agents take risk on behalf of the organization and manage the associated exposures. However, the broad reference to 'risk culture' and the 'tone at the top' falls short of providing definitions and clear prescriptions on how to implement this in practice.

Here alternative perspectives from the management field can provide useful insights about the role of structures, processes, and human agency influenced by cultural artifacts and behaviors that are conducive to effective responses as various risk events occur. Parts of the operations management literature are preoccupied with the ability to construe effective supply chains where different inputs are sourced, combined, and distributed to end-users delivering the right outputs, in the proper places, and at the right time points, thereby uncovering relevant structural dimensions. So, by setting up, or designing, more flexible value-chain configurations, the resources can be engaged across a structured business network that is conducive to effective adaptation when unexpected events and developments arise. Whereas a loop-sided focus on value-chain optimization is likely to increase vulnerability to disruptions, a flexible value-chain, or network, will be more agile and adaptive. This introduces the concept of resilience as the ability of a value network to adapt toward new more desirable structures after major disturbances and not just revert to an original form (Christopher and Peck, 2004). In other words, resilience reflects an organizational ability to adjust to changing conditions and emerge in a stronger state better adapted to the evolving conditions going forward (Annarelli and Nonino, 2016).

There is also increasing evidence to suggest that the ability to engage in fast managerial responses after a major incidence, or disaster event, is a more effective approach than waiting to obtain monetary compensation, for example, from insurance covers for direct losses. Hence, the ability to communicate with honesty responding with local care and efficiency generally commands a substantial value recovery premium, particularly after mass fatality events irrespective of their causes (Knight and Pretty, 2005). Insurance can provide a financial cover for direct economic losses caused by predefined risks as the means to replace the damaged assets, but the direct economic loss may only be a small part of the impact. The longer-term indirect, or secondary, economic effects may in reality be (much more) substantial. Hence, the installation of better structures and processes for disaster preparedness and recovery can be more beneficial than replacement of assets (Hallegatte and Dumas, 2009). Recent experiences suggest that organizations can achieve faster economic recovery within a dynamic functional network where direct interaction and collective decisions with local actors can shape a more successful economic recovery (Seville et al., 2015).

Consciously building and engaging in collaborative stakeholder relationships in the local regions where the organization is operating seems instrumental for the ability to foster diverse and creative solutions to new emerging events and developments. To that effect, it is important to better understand how the organization, and its senior management, can support the formation of relevant network relationships and retain an open and receptive environment where insights and experiences from the core stakeholder connections can be considered. For example, Shoemaker and Day (2009) suggest that the ability to sense 'weak signals from the periphery' closer to the various stakeholders is an important quality in responsive organizations. All the while, they note that "organizations get blindsided not so much because decision makers aren't seeing signals, but because they jump to the most convenient or plausible conclusion" (p. 82). In other words, psychological and cognitive biases are at play that make individual decision-makers interpret the surroundings in particular ways that fit conveniently with their own predominant worldview, which causes otherwise clear signals to be ignored or dismissed, thereby leaving the organization unprepared for the next major event.

In this context, we can also learn from studies of 'high reliability organizations' where the individual organizational agents focus on the potential for failure, remain attentive to operations, favor complete explanations, and prioritize individual expertise (e.g., Weick and Sutcliffe, 2001). Hence, the reliability of diverse, complex, networked organizations exposed to rapidly changing conditions with different institutional preferences depends on the engagement of, and interaction among, a group of diverse 'reliability professionals' (Schulman et al., 2016). So, forming an organizational culture where individual qualities and insights have preference should enable more responsive and adaptive organizations that are better at dealing with uncertain and unexpected circumstances.

This further suggests that responsible corporate behavior can build strong stakeholder relationships and create a reputation as a reliable counterpart, which can help the organization develop viable solutions to unexpected and complex crises situations should they occur (e.g., Andersen, 2017). Husted (2005) finds that acting in line with the principles of corporate (social) responsibility is associated with lower risk and higher returns as firms proactively consider broader stakeholder and social effects and thereby anticipate major risks that otherwise might be overlooked. Hence, the engagement in corporate responsible initiatives may create forward-looking projects that represent operational flexibilities and potential business solutions with real option features that can enhance the SRM capabilities (Husted, 2005). Whereas major multinational firms typically try to counterweigh effects of high levels of country-specific and sovereign risks by increasing the discount rate in their cross-border investment propositions, many of them also use local partnership structures as a way to deal proactively with local political risks (Holmen and Pramborg, 2009). Similarly, it is argued that multinational enterprise can manage risk in particularly fragile and conflict-affected regions by adopting collaborative strategies that reduce investment risk and create stability and prosperity in the local community as opposed to reacting to risk events as they occur (Oetzel and Miklian, 2017).

Strategic decisions should arguably consider all the relevant ethical concerns. As Weitzner and Darroch (2009) noted, "greater attention needs to be paid to the issues of strategic goals, risk assessments related to stakeholders, boundaries between public and private concerns, and managerial decisions" (p. 363). The decision-makers in contemporary organizations are under considerable pressure to show good performance and avoid major crisis situations in highly complex and volatile business environments that can derail things. This is where ERM might come in with a holistic integrative risk approach to complement strategic planning with an aim of preparing for potential events identifying, assessing, and mitigating major risks and possibly support responsive risk management capabilities. However, rational risk analyses do not account for behavioral norms, or values, needed to form a responsive organization, but only performs calculative exercises to assess potential consequences. Therefore, "ethics trumps strategy in a world where undecidable positions are a fact of life" (Weitzner and Darroch, 2009, p. 371) and the ethical priorities should be an engrained part of the organizational culture.

Human biases and behavior

A recent review of the ERM literature notes that "accounting and finance scholars often define optimal conditions, and then offer tools consistent with those conditions" whereas "management scholars emphasize understanding how firms behave" (Bromiley et al., 2014, p. 273). This reflects an underlying belief that adoption of a formal ERM framework automatically delivers the promised outcomes where the effects instead might depend on the way the risk management processes interact with the organizational context and complex strategy-making activities. Hence, there is an important role for strategic management scholars to consider how the formal risk practices relate to the dynamics of organizational strategy-making through strategic planning and emergent strategic responses in the face of a changing environment. The principles of ERM imply that major risks can be identified (up front), assessed, and managed on an ongoing basis while exposures (and the status of risk initiatives) are monitored in control-based reporting at different organizational levels. However, this stylized practice can make it difficult to handle unexpected events when they arise, which is where the interplay with strategic planning and emergent responses might come into the fore. Hence, there are many examples of organizations that implemented an ERM framework, yet failed to circumvent major operational incidents or deal in time with emergent life-threatening strategic challenges or issues.

For example, Nokia was once the most successful first-mover in mobile phones and became the dominant producer in 2007, where almost half of all mobile phones were produced by Nokia, whereas Apple iPhones only made up 5% of the market (e.g., Andersen, 2018). However, the iPhone paved the way for new smartphones that disrupted the existing market order and where Nokia, for some reason, was incapable of adapting to the change, leading to a gradual deterioration of prior market dominance. The decay was so complete that Nokia's entire mobile phone business was sold to Microsoft only seven years later at a fraction of the prior market valuation. Interestingly, Nokia had risk policies in place using state-of-the-art risk management tools reporting relevant exposures into the risk governance process. A dedicated risk management function looked at financial, operational, and strategic risks that could prevent Nokia from reaching its business objectives. Yet, these practices did little to circumvent the downfall of Nokia's mobile phone business, possibly because the cognitive biases of senior managers prevented them from forming a balanced judgment in their strategic decision-making.

On March 11, 2011, Japan was hit by a 9.0 Richter scale earthquake with an epicenter 130 km east of Sendai in North-Eastern Honshû. The aftershocks produced a 14-meter tsunami that affected the nuclear power plant operated by Tokyo Electric Power Company (TEPCO). The earthquake halted the power supply to the cooling systems for the boiling water reactors (BWR) and led to a release of radioactive substances. The tsunami that hit an hour later caused major damages to the pumps and stopped the emergency diesel-fueled generators. Attempts to install mobile emergency generators failed due to lack of proper cable connections and rising temperatures caused an explosion in reactor 1 on March 12, followed by an explosion in reactor 3 on March 13, and a final meltdown of reactor 2 on March 15. Prior to this, TEPCO had a history of bad incidents with false reporting and concealment of safety issues that led to a complete governance overhaul in 2002, where a new board took measures to ensure that similar incidents would never happen again. Stronger corporate ethics and compliance requirements were imposed to ensure transparency about nuclear operations, including implementing a risk management framework to identify and evaluate group-wide risks that might affect group operations. The chairman of the committee reporting on the incidence noted that despite the formal risk management practices, people will not see things they do not wish to see, but only see what they wish to see and, therefore, a risk framework alone does not mean it will function (TNDJ, 2012).

An explosion at BP's Texas City refinery on March 23, 2005, killed 15 workers and injured more than 170 people. The subsequent Baker Report (2007) found that BP did not show effective process safety leadership with process safety established as a core value. They found instances of a slack operating discipline with serious deviations from safe practices and apparent complacency toward process safety (Baker Report, 2007). Hence, John Brown retired prematurely as CEO on May 1, 2007, before the release of the Baker Report (2007) and Tony Heyward became new CEO with a mandate to improve things going forward. To this end, BP (among other things) introduced a code of conduct where the first item stressed BP's emphasis on health, safety, security, and the environment to protect the communities where the company operates and the people working for them. So, genuine initiatives were taken to turn things around in the organization while obviously still having to deal with the relentless executive demands to persevere in a highly competitive global business. Nevertheless, on April 20, 2010, some three years later, the Deepwater Horizon rig commissioned by BP in the Mexican Gulf exploded killing 11 crewmen and igniting a fireball that was visible 35 miles away. The fire could not be extinguished, and the rig sank after two days with a leaking well at the seabed causing the largest offshore oil spill in US history (e.g., Andersen and Andersen, 2014).

In short, there is plenty of case-based 'real-life' evidence to suggest that adoption of an ERM framework and associated formal practices will not provide any guarantee that the organization is better positioned to deal with major operational and strategic risks. Similarly, establishing an official code of conduct provides little comfort that the organization is operating in line with the proposed guidelines. Many other relevant factors are at play including the effects of human psychology and social behaviors where the extant management scholarship can provide essential insights to advance our understanding about effective handling of strategic risks. The evidence similarly illustrates the difficulties associated with the establishment of ethical and responsible organizational cultures, even when the leadership is acting in good faith, because old habits, views, and priorities remain engrained in the daily behaviors. Hence, more research efforts, and more nuanced research efforts at that, are needed to better understand these dynamics in the context of prevailing views on ERM.

Add to this, a better understanding of the risk reporting within organizations that typically originates from frontline managers and then travels to the general management and governance levels, providing an overview of existing and emergent exposures. However, it is observed how actions typically do not automatically follow from the reporting, so the risk reports can change in tone and content as vehicles to encourage needed action (Christiansen and Thrane, 2014). In contrast, COSO (2004) implicitly assumes that organizational actions will follow in line with the reported risk mitigation initiatives. Hence, commenting on qualitative studies of risk reports in financial institutions, Mikes (2009) identifies distinctly different types of reporting and argues that a 'quantitative skeptical' approach creates more attention to risk matters than a 'quantitative enthusiast' approach. This all suggest that risk reports are used as means of communication between organizational levels and that there is a human-based dynamic inherent in the reporting processes that influence the way the organization and its individual agents deal with and respond to risks. We obviously need to know more about these aspects.

Uncertainty and extreme events

The globalization of private and public organizations, individual social links across societies, cross-border flows of goods, services, and information with a promise of ongoing digital enhancement all contribute to form complex living network relationships that increase uncertainty in the business environment. It can be understood as a dynamic complex system comprised by many interacting agents and entities where outcomes defeat simple comprehension because the behavior of each component depends on the behavior of other components. Hence, the eventual outcomes cannot just be derived from a simple aggregation of individual behaviors because they are interdependent and can have nonlinear effects. Since events and responses to them follow irreversible paths, that is, they cannot be reversed – what has happened has happened – decisions must be made along the way to determine the direction the path will take. In this context, it is not possible to forecast events and developments because things are intertwined in intricate networks of interacting elements. The increasing uncertainty challenges conventional risk management approaches that are based on assumptions of risk as (identifiable and) quantifiable uncertainty, whereas (true) uncertainty cannot be quantified (Knight, 1921). All the while, many interacting components of a dynamic complex system often assume properties of power laws with extreme effects. These conditions obviously impose new demands on our ability to manage strategic risks in organizations that operate in multinational contexts or are exposed to global influences.

The introduction of the 'black-swan' concept denotes the observed occurrence of extreme events as an essential aspect of contemporary life (Taleb, 2007a). It also notes that humans tend to ignore the role of randomness and large deviations that contravene the norms of scientific approaches by continuing to rely on large-scale predictions to assess future conditions. Nonetheless, we are – and always have been – exposed to rare and improbable events that defeat the common risk management principles, and they may now exert more influence than we care to realize. These black-swan events may be particularly impactful exactly because we tend to ignore them, so they become unexpected or otherwise 'predictable surprises' (Bazerman and Watkins, 2004). Humans at all levels of the hierarchy have a propensity to extrapolate prior experiences onto future events, even though what we believe we know from past experience may be an illusion particularly as the environment becomes more uncertain and unpredictable. In this context, the black-swan phenomenon is critical of all-purpose use of statistics, arguing that blind adherence to statistical numbers and metrics can reduce risk awareness and healthy skepticism. This becomes particularly critical in fat-tailed domains where conventional statistical measures cease to have any practical meaning, but rather has the potential to misrepresent the true exposures. So, the black swan is intended to create cognition around the importance of tail events and make us realize the areas where we have limited knowledge. As Taleb (2007b) argues, "it is impossible to make precise statements about unseen events, those that lie outside the sample set, we need to make the richest possible scenarios about them" (p. 2). In other words, there is a need to know more about how we can deal with the black-swan events in the tails that often represent the real strategic risks with large potential upsides and downsides.

The extensive literature on decision theory and choice under uncertainty has typically been limited to situations where we can claim to know a given probability distribution of possible risk outcomes that ignore the possibility of fat tail events. The black-swan events refer to the so-called 'fourth quadrant' where the forecast errors are large and the effects of outcomes consequential, which represent the types of events that require a more cautious treatment (Taleb, 2009). The simple problem is that a black-swan event, say, the effects of a 100-year crisis, will never be part of the statistical sample, which, in many cases, only goes back a few years or, possibly, decades. According to Taleb (2009), "it takes much, much longer for a fat-tailed time series to reveal its properties – in fact, many can, in short episodes, masquerade as thin-tailed" (p. 757). So, part of the problem is that conventional risk management frameworks apply tools that are misguided to deal with uncertainty and extreme events and we need more research to focus on this issue, its consequences for practice, and possible remedies.

Discourse and institutionalization

We can then ask ourselves why the general principles of ERM have been extended to deal with all types of uncertainties, both quantifiable and unquantifiable, where the latter applies more to strategic risk phenomena that are often unique when they occur and therefore defeat simple quantification. Part of the answer to this question is that particular views and professions have forcefully promoted particular approaches with little (initially at least) consideration for alternative interpretations. Hence, it is argued that the accounting field has claimed an expanded mandate "as high status actors" with a higher focus on financial audit that creates "a climate of fiscal constraint, shifting the locus of oversight power from bureaucratic elites to financially minded managers" (Power, 2003, p. 188). This increased emphasis on financial audit moved the focus toward oversight of performance-related measures, including cost-effectiveness, where the audit function relates to 'auditable' financial concepts. Therefore, the auditing role has increasingly become that of "an explicit change agent, rather than just a verifier" (Power, 2003, pp. 188–189) in line with quality control frameworks like ISO and others. As a consequence, it has created management control systems where auditing is enforcing "regulatory systems that prescribe frameworks of internal control and self-management for regulated organizations" (Power, 2003, p. 189) with an emphasis on compliance. These general observations predict the emergence of formal monitoring institutions that transfer power to auditing bodies on a wide range of issues, including the ability to set strategies and ensure fulfillment of strategic objectives, which is exactly what the dominant standard setting ERM frameworks are doing.

The literature on discourse and power can help explain how these circumstances arise. Discourse is defined as sets of interrelated texts and practices that over time systematically shape a common meaning on a given subject, so the discourse can form a specific conceptual understanding of risk and its organization among those involved in the related communication process (Hardy and Maguire, 2016). The discourse produces specific meanings about what is considered to be normal, standard, and acceptable, thereby institutionalizing particular practices and behaviors. However, a discursive process is more than just a common way of seeing things it also exerts its own power by reproducing that particular way of seeing as being the truth (Knights and Morgan, 1991). Hardy and Maguire (2016) observe different ways to conceptualize the risk organization depending on whether the aim is to manage future risks, real-time risk events, or past risk situations where ERM frameworks traditionally have been mostly concerned with assessment of future risks. However, a too one-sided adoption of a specific risk perspective can provide an incomplete view of all relevant aspects of the risk management challenge. As Hardy and Maguire (2016) argue, it is common to organize risk management by implementing expert risk knowledge from past empirical information that is "abstracted into regularities in the form of plans, scripts, and protocols" (p. 89). However, these approaches are less effective when dealing with risk events that deviate from expectations and the organization is faced with unknown conditions. Hence, there is a need to not only adopt approaches that draw on traditional risk knowledge from the past but also draw "attention to discontinuity and uncertainty in knowledge about risk" (Hardy and Maguire, 2016, p. 87).

Interaction with strategy

The prevalent ERM standards like COSO and ISO are in principle accessible for everyone that want to buy the blueprints and use them to implement the ERM framework or hire consultants to help with the process. However, the general access to standardized practices contravenes the fundamental assumptions of the resource-based view (RBV) where sustainable competitive advantage (SCA) derives from unique firm-specific organizational processes that are hard to imitate (e.g., Barney, 1986a, b, 1991). In contrast, a practice-based view (PBV) of strategy suggests that properly adopted standard practices may enhance management effectiveness (Bromiley and Rau, 2014). This is obviously a potential theoretical contradiction in strategic management as PBV argues that formal practices can have performance effects whereas RBV argues that this is not possible because it violates the rarity and inimitability conditions. The publicly accessible and widely prescribed ERM practices should not provide conditions for imperfect imitation required to gain sustainable advantages. Yet, PBV argues that standard practices can enhance performance, for example, from improved managerial decision-making in line with a strategy-as-practice view where strategy derives from something organizations do (e.g., Johnson et al., 2007). The conflicting predictions of RBV and PBV can be uncovered through empirical testing, the current inconclusive status of which is discussed elsewhere.

However, the PBV approach opens for the possibility of assessing ERM practices in the context of basic strategy-making processes as possible proxies for SRM-like conditions where, for example, interaction with mediating and moderating strategy-making processes may influence the effects of ERM. This suggests that some organizations have unique interactive capabilities between ERM practices and general strategy-making processes that are value-creating and hard to imitate. If the interactive competencies represent causal ambiguity that is hard to emulate by outsiders, it can be a source of competitive advantage that assumes SCA characteristics if those competencies are renewed through ongoing investment (King and Zeithaml, 2001; Lippman and Rumelt, 1982; Reed and DeFilippi, 1990). The ability to deploy firm-specific strategy-making processes and use interactive capabilities to integrate with the ERM practices can provide a basis for causal ambiguity as support for SCA, even though ERM practices are standardized.

This would argue that adopting ERM frameworks by itself cannot guarantee SCA effects, something else must be added, such as an ability to integrate with existing strategy-making processes that could have better ways of handling emergent treats and opportunities, where ERM focuses on the handling of identified risks. This also links to the current debate about dynamic capabilities, that is, the ability to adapt the strategy to changing conditions, where Eisenhardt and Martin (2000) argue that dynamic capabilities constitute best practices or common routines that challenge their unique value-creating potential. Instead, they argue that SCA derives from an ability to construe new competitive resource configurations that respond to the changing competitive landscape (Eisenhardt and Martin, 2000). This in turn may be linked to a structure where simple routines and more complex interactive routines operate in unison displayed in interaction between ERM practices and different strategy-making processes in a dynamic bundle of competencies (Peteraf, Di Stefano and Verona, 2013).

Policy-making effects

The powerful implications of discourse seems nowhere as clearly displayed as in the context of the adoption of ERM frameworks where the empirical evidence on their effects remains ambiguous with a need for more thorough and nuanced research results. However, the professional risk management field has strong proponents to endorse the ERM practices, arguing that a holistic approach creates positive synergies and reduces duplication of efforts (FERMA/ECIIA, 2011).[1] Another rationale is that aligning internal risk limits (and an expressed risk appetite) with the organization's strategic goals will reduce expected losses and increase the likelihood of achieving expected returns (FERMA/ECIIA, 2014). While these claims might have theoretical substance, there are few, if any, studies to demonstrate that these conditions will automatically arise from adoption of ERM, and if not, showing what the contingencies are for it to happen. Despite a lack of clear evidence, the ERM approach is promoted by regulators that argue for legally binding rules as better procedural risk governance safeguards (Arndorfer and Minto, 2015). In accordance with this, the Basel Committee on Banking Supervision (BCBS) has issued corporate governance guidelines (2015) recommending these procedures that are similarly condoned by the Organization for Economic Co-operation and Development (OECD) and the European Commission (EC). The various writings and reports released on the subject of ERM as a foundation for the risk governance rules within the European Union (EU) emphasizing management control, internal audit, and financial regulation illustrates the self-re-enforcing emergence of key concepts among engaged constituents.

Hence, ERM has gradually become the linchpin for risk governance particularly in the regulated financial sector, reflecting a belief in formal risk management practices to support managers assessing the risks of key decisions based on compliance (e.g., Srivastav and Hagendorff, 2016). The ERM approach has been extended into a three-lines-of-defense (TLD) model as a more comprehensive way of helping management govern enterprise risks and sustain value-creation. The TLD model is considered entirely consistent with the formal COSO risk management framework and thus has evolved as a natural outgrowth from the formal ERM frameworks (Anderson and Eubanks, 2015). The first line of defense constitutes the frontline operational activities where local risk management committees supposedly make regular reports and minutes from business unit risk committee meetings (Doughty, 2011). The second line of defense constitutes compliance and risk oversight functions that report to the management and board risk committee. The third line is the independent reviews of internal and external auditors as a retrospective process for improvement. Lyons (2011) suggests that each line of defense assumes specific risk responsibilities linked to their organizational functions, arguing that the 2008 financial crisis was exacerbated by failed risk oversight of boards and executive teams.

The TLD model is supposed to coordinate the ERM-based risk management processes in ways that create administrative efficiencies where the risk control functions are integrated to avoid gaps and omissions while ensuring that various efforts are not duplicated (IIA, 2013). The operational management functions execute the daily business activities and manage those risks in the first line of defense. The supervisory controls for executive management and the board constitute the second line of defense to ensure that the organization complies with regulation, note process inadequacies, potential breakdowns, and unexpected developments (ECIIA, 2013; IIA, 2013). The TLD model is promoted by financial regulators and academic proponents, arguing that corporate governance failures contributed to the 2008 financial crisis prompting a need for board-level risk procedures safeguarded by legally binding rules (Arndorfer and Minto, 2015). Hence, the corporate governance guidelines issued by the BCBS (BIS, 2015) proposed that bank risk procedures should be organized around an independent function headed by a chief risk officer (CRO). This idea was similarly promoted by the OECD and a corporate governance green paper on financial institutions by the EC. The argument is that the boards of financial institution are inadequate with an insufficient understanding of risk and a lack of real-time risk information.

The ERM-based TLD model has then become the benchmark for reformed internal control systems in financial institutions as the proper way to assign control and risk management responsibilities. Nonetheless, the existing empirical studies on ERM performance fail to unequivocally demonstrate the promised effects and very few studies have investigated whether the effectiveness benefits associated with the TLD model actually materialize. There is similarly little knowledge about the effects of CROs, what their roles are, and the specific circumstances required for these functions to have any durable effect on organizational outcomes. This seems to point toward an urgent need to conduct more detailed studies to discern the role of ERM practices and TLD approaches to better understand the organizational contexts and conditions that may be associated with an ability to manage strategic risks that can make or break the organizations whether or not they are a financial institution.

In conclusion, SRM is a multidisciplinary and rather fractured field of study characterized by prevalent ERM approaches as vehicles to handle all types of risks where SRM provides more nuanced views as a prerequisite for dealing effectively with emergent strategic exposures. The review of a fairly broad extant literature that can be reasonably linked to SRM points to often overlooked influences of values and ethics embedded in organizational norms and related influences of human biases and social behaviors that affect the ability to observe change and respond to it. A number of research streams in management studies, organizational behavior, psychology, and sociology can provide valuable insights to extend our understanding of ERM practices and their effects on the ability to deal with strategic risks. It is noted how uncertainty seems to emerge as an increasing and unavoidable challenge to be dealt with that can lead to extreme events and falling short of the conventional risk management paradigm, thus calling for new approaches to deal with dynamic complex environments. Part of the answer to this challenge may be found in more extensive studies of the interaction between ERM practices and strategy-making processes as the basis for dynamic adaptive organizations. Finally, we observe the powerful influence of discourse and policy-making initiatives that needs stronger empirical support to provide legislative prescriptions. This suggests a research agenda with studies that are more sensitive to the human elements, including behavioral artifacts, cognitive biases and limitations, and the significance of responsible behavior, broader stakeholder concerns with collaborative long-term strategic solutions for the common good. It also reveals a potential conundrum between evidence-based initiatives and policy-making driven by the power of public discourse and institutional forces where more research is needed to enhance our ability to deal with the major strategic exposures of our time.

Note

1 The joint recommendation was endorsed by European Confederation of Institutes of Internal Auditing (ECIIA) and Federation of European Risk Management Associations (FERMA) as a guide to boards and audit committees when complying with Article 41.2 of the 8th EU Company Law Directive (DIRECTIVE 2006/43/EC – Art. 41–2b), which requires that "the audit committee shall, inter alia: monitor the effectiveness of the company's internal control, internal audit where applicable, and risk management systems."

References

Abernethy, M. A. and Brownell, P. (1999). The role of budgets in organizations facing strategic change: an exploratory study, *Accounting, Organizations and Society*, 24(3), 189–204.

Adner, R. and Helfat, C. E. (2003). Corporate effects and dynamic managerial capabilities, *Strategic Management Journal*, 24, 1011–1025.

Aguilar, F. J. (1967). *Scanning the Business Environment*. Macmillan, New York, NY.

Aleisa, Y. (2018). Factors affecting implementation of enterprise risk management: An exploratory study among Saudi organizations, *Journal of Economics, Business and Management*, 6(1), doi: 10.18178/joebm.2018.6.1.543

Al-Najjar, B. and Taylor, P. (2008). The relationship between capital structure and ownership structure: New evidence from Jordanian panel data, *Managerial Finance*, 34(12), 919–933.

Alviniussen, A. and Jankensgard, H. (2009). Enterprise risk budgeting: Bringing risk management into the financial planning process, *Journal of Applied Finance*, 19(1/2), 178–190.

Anderson, D. J. and Eubanks, G. (2015). Leveraging COSO across the three lines of defense. The Institute of International Auditors, Committee of Sponsoring Organizations of the Treadway Commission (COSO). [www.coso.org/Documents/COSO-2015-3LOD.pdf]

Andersen, T. J. (2000). Strategic planning, autonomous actions and corporate performance, *Long Range Planning*, 33(2), 184–200.

Andersen, T. J. (2004). Integrating decentralized strategy making and strategic planning processes in dynamic environments, *Journal of Management Studies*, 41(8), 1271–1299.

Andersen, T. J. (2008). The performance relationship of effective risk management: Exploring the firm-specific investment rationale, *Long Range Planning*, 41(2), 155–176.

Andersen, T. J. (2009). Effective risk management outcomes: Exploring effects of innovation and capital structure, *Journal of Strategy and Management*, 2(4), 352–379.

Andersen, T. J. (2011). The risk implications of multinational enterprise. *International Journal of Organizational Analysis*, 19(1), 49–70.

Andersen, T. J. (2012). Multinational risk and performance outcomes: Effects of knowledge intensity and industry context, *International Business Review*, 21(2), 239–252.

Andersen, T. J. (2015). Strategic adaptation. In Wright, J. D. (ed.), *International Encyclopedia of the Social & Behavioral Sciences*. Elsevier, Amsterdam, The Netherlands, 501–507.

Andersen, T. J. (ed.) (2016). *The Routledge Companion to Strategic Risk Management*. Routledge, Abingdon, Oxon, UK.

Andersen, T. J. (2017). Corporate responsible behavior in multinational enterprise, *International Journal of International Analysis*, 25(3), 1–21.

Andersen, T. J. (2018). *Nokia – The Rise and Fall of an Icon. Case,* Copenhagen Business School, Frederiksberg, Denmark.

Andersen, T. J. and Andersen, C. B. (2014). *British Petroleum: From Texas City to the Gulf of Mexico and Beyond*. Case Centre Reference No. 714–017-1. Case, Copenhagen Business School, Frederiksberg, Denmark.

Andersen, T. J., Denrell, J. and Bettis, R. A. (2007). Strategic responsiveness and Bowman's risk–return paradox, *Strategic Management Journal*, 28(4), 407–429.

Andersen, T. J., Garvey, M. and Roggi, O. (2014). *Managing Risk and Opportunity*. Oxford University Press, Oxford, UK.

Andersen, T. J. and Nielsen, B. B. (2009). Adaptive strategy making: The effects of emergent and intended strategy modes, *European Management Review*, 6(2), 94–106.

Andersen T. J. and Schrøder P. W. (2010). *Strategic Risk Management Practice: How to Deal Effectively with Major Corporate Exposures*. Cambridge University Press, Cambridge, UK.

Andrews, K. R. (1987). *The Concept of Corporate Strategy* (custom edition), McGraw-Hill, New York, NY (first published in 1971).

Annarelli, A. and Nonino, F. (2016). Strategic and operational management of organizational resilience, *Omega*, 62, 1–18.

Ansoff, H. I. (1980). Strategic issue management. *Strategic Management Journal*, 1, 131–148.

Ansoff, H. I. (1984). *Implanting Strategic Management*. Prentice-Hall, Englewood Cliffs, NJ.

Ansoff, H. I. (1987). *Corporate Strategy* (update edition). Penguin Books, London, UK (first published in 1965).

Ansoff, H. I. (1988). *The New Corporate Strategy*. Wiley, New York, NY.

Anthony, R. (1965). *Planning and Control Systems: A Framework for Analysis*. Division of Research, Graduate School of Business Administration, Harvard University, Boston, MA.

Arndorfer I. and Minto A. (2015). The "four" lines of defence model" for financial institutions. Financial Stability Institute, Occasional Paper No. 11, Bank for International Settlements (BIS), Basel, Switzerland. [www.bis.org/fsi/fsipapers11.pdf]

AS/NZS 4360. (2004). Australian/New Zealand Standard AS/NZS 4360:2004: Risk Management. Standards Australia, Homebush, NSW and Standards New Zealand, Wellington.

Ashford, S. J., Rothbard, N. P., Piderit, S. K. and Dutton, J. E. (1998). Out on a limb: The role of context and impression management in selling gender-equity issues, *Administrative Science Quarterly*, 43(1), 23–57.

Baird, I. S. and Thomas, H. (1985). Toward a contingency model of strategic risk taking. *Academy of Management Review*, 10, 230–243.

Baker Report. (2007). The Report of the BP U.S. Refineries Independent Safety Review Panel. [http://sunnyday.mit.edu/Baker-panel-report.pdf]

Banbury, C. and Hart, S. (1994). How strategy-making processes can make a difference. *Strategic Management Journal*, 15, 251–269.

Barney, J. B. (1986a). Strategic factor markets: Expectations, luck, and business strategy, *Management Science*, 32(10), 1231–1241.

Barney, J. B. (1986b). Organizational culture: Can it be a source of sustained competitive advantage? *Academy of Management Review*, 11(3), 656–665.

Barney, J. B. (1991). Firm resources and sustained competitive advantage, *Journal of Management*, 17(1), 99–120.

Barr, P. S. (1998). Adapting to unfamiliar environmental events: A look at the evolution of interpretation and its role in strategic change, *Organization Science*, 9(6), 644–669.

Barton, T. L., Shenkir, W. G. and Walker, P. L. (2002). *Making Enterprise Risk Management Pay Off*. Financial Times/Prentice Hall, Upper Saddle River, NJ.

Baxter, R., Bedard, J. C., Hoitash, R. and Yezegel, A. (2013). Enterprise risk management program quality: Determinants, value relevance, and the financial crisis, *Contemporary Accounting Research*, 30(4), 1264–1295.

Bazerman, M. H. and Watkins, M. D. (2004). *Predictable Surprises: The Disasters You Should Have Seen Coming*. Harvard Business School Press, Boston, MA.

Beasley, M. S., Branson, B. C. and Hancock, B. V. (2012). Current State of Enterprise Risk Oversight: Progress Is Occurring But Opportunities for Improvement Remain. American Institute of Certified Public Accountants (AICPA). [https://erm.ncsu.edu/az/erm/i/chan/library/AICPA_ERM_Research_Study_ 2012.pdf]

Beasley, M. S., Branson, B. C. and Hancock, B. V. (2016). 2016 The State of Risk Oversight: An Overview of Enterprise Risk Management Practices. American Institute of Certified Public Accountants (AICPA). [https://erm.ncsu.edu/az/erm/i/chan/library/AICPA_ERM_Research_Study_2016.pdf]

Beasley, M. S., Branson, B. and Pagach, D. (2015). An analysis of the maturity and strategic impact of investments in ERM, *Journal of Accounting and Public Policy*, 34, 219–243.

Beasley, M. S., Clune, R. and Hermanson, D. R. (2005). Enterprise risk management: An empirical analysis of factors associated with the extent of implementation, *Journal of Accounting and Public Policy*, 24(6), 521–531.

Beasley, M. S. and Frigo, M. L. (2010). ERM and its role in strategic planning and strategy execution. In Fraser, J. and Simkins, B. (eds.), *Enterprise Risk Management: Today's Leading Research and Best Practices for Tomorrow's Executives*, 31–50. doi:10.1002/9781118267080.ch3

Beasley, M. S., Pagach, D. and Warr, R. (2008). Information conveyed in hiring announcements of senior executives overseeing enterprise-wide risk management processes, *Journal of Accounting, Auditing & Finance*, 23(3), 311–332.

Beck, U. (1992). *Risk Society: Towards a New Modernity*. Sage, Thousand Oaks, CA.

Berry-Stoelzle, T. R. and Xu, J. (2018). Enterprise risk management and the cost of capital, *Journal of Risk and Insurance*, 85(1), 159–201.

Bettis, R. A. (1983). Modern financial theory, corporate strategy and public policy: Three conundrums, *The Academy of Management Review*, 8(3), 406–415.

Bettis, R. A. and Hitt, M. A. (1995). The new competitive landscape, *Strategic Management Journal*, 16(S1), 7–19.

Bettis, R. A. and Mahajan, V. (1985). Risk/return performance of diversified firms, *Management Science*, 31(7), 785–918.

Bettis, R. A. and Thomas, H. (1990). *Risk, Strategy, and Management*. JAI Press, Greenwich, CT.

BIS. (2015). Guidelines – Corporate Governance Principles for Banks, Basel Committee on Banking Supervision, Bank for International Settlement (BIS). [www.bis.org/bcbs/publ/d328.pdf]

Bisbe, J. and Otley, D. (2004). The effects of the interactive use of management control systems on product innovation, *Accounting, Organizations and Society*, 29(8), 709–737.

Bohnert, A., Gatzert, N., Hoyt, R. E. and Lechner, P. (2019). The drivers and value of enterprise risk management: Evidence from ERM ratings, *The European Journal of Finance*, 25(3), 234–255. doi:10.1080/1351847X.2018.1514314

Bower, J. L. and Noda, T. (1996). Strategy making as iterated processes, *Strategic Management Journal*, 17, 159–192.

Bowman, E. H. (1980). A risk–return paradox for strategic management, *Sloan Management Review*, 21, 17–31.

Bowman, E. H. (1984). Content analysis of annual reports for corporate strategy and risk, *Interfaces*, 14(1), 61–71.

Boyd, B. K. (1991). Strategic planning and financial performance: A meta-analytic review, *Journal of Management Studies*, 28(4), 353–374.

Boyd, B. K. and Reuning-Elliott, E. (1998). A measurement model of strategic planning, *Strategic Management Journal*, 19, 181–192.

Braumann, E. C. (2018). Analyzing the role of risk awareness in enterprise risk management, *Journal of Management Accounting Research*, 30(20), 241–268.

Brealey, R. A., Myers, S. C. and Allen, F. (2011). *Fundamentals of Corporate Finance*. McGraw-Hill Irwin, New York, NY. (first edition in 1980).

Brews, P. J. and Hunt, M. R. (1999). Learning to plan and planning to learn: Resolving the planning school/learning school debate, *Strategic Management Journal*, 20, 889–913.

Bromiley, P. (1991). Testing a causal model of corporate risk taking and performance, *Academy of Management Journal*, 34(1), 37–59.

Bromiley, P., McShane, M., Nair, A. and Rustambekov, E. (2014). Enterprise risk management: Review, critique, and research directions, *Long Range Planning*, 48(4), 265–276.

Bromiley, P. and Rau, D. (2014). Towards a practice-based view of strategy, *Strategic Management Journal*, 35, 1249–1256.

Bromiley, P., Rau, D. and McShane, M. (2016). Can strategic risk management contribute to enterprise risk management? In Andersen, T. J. (ed.), *The Routledge Companion to Strategic Risk Management*. Routledge, Abingdon, Oxon, UK, 140–156.

Brown, S. L. and Eisenhardt, K. M. (1997). The art of continuous change: Linking complexity theory and time-paced evolution in relentlessly shifting organizations, *Administrative Science Quarterly*, 42(1), 1–34.

Bruining, H., Bonnet, M. and Wright, M. (2004). Management control systems and strategy change in buyouts, *Management Accounting Research*, 15(2), 155–177.

BSI. (2007). *Specification for Business Continuity Management [BS 25999-2]*. The British Standards Institution (BSI), London, UK.

Burchell, S., Clubb, C., Hopwood, A., Hughes, J. and Nahapiet, J. (1980). The roles of accounting in organizations and society, *Accounting, Organizations and Society*, 5(1), 5–27.

Burgelman, R. A. (1983). Corporate entrepreneurship and strategic management: Insights from a process study, *Management Science*, 29(12), 1349–1364.

Burgelman, R. A. and Grove, A. (1996). Strategic dissonance, *California Management Review*, 38(2), 8–28.

Burgelman, R. A. and Grove, A. (2007). Let chaos reign, then rein in chaos—repeatedly: managing strategic dynamics for corporate longevity, *Strategic Management Journal*, 28(19), 965–979.

Burns, J. and Vaivio, J. (2001). Management accounting change, *Management Accounting Research*, 12(4), 389–402.

Callahan, C. and Soileau, J. (2017). Does enterprise risk management enhance operating performance? *Advances in Accounting, incorporating Advances in International Accounting.* doi:10.1016/j.adiac.2017.01.001

Camillus, J. C. (1975). Evaluating the benefits of formal planning systems, *Long Range Planning*, 8(3), 33–40.

Capon, N., Fakley, U. and Hulbert, M. (1994). Strategic planning and financial performance: More evidence, *Journal of Management Studies*, 33(1), 105–110.

Carse, D. (1999). Mr. Carse speak about the regulatory framework of e-banking. *BIS Review* 108/1999, 1–6. Keynote Speech at the Symposium on Applied R&D.

CAS. (2003, May). Overview of Enterprise Risk Management. Enterprise Risk Management Committee. Casualty Actuarial Society (CAS). [www.casact.org/research/erm/overview.pdf.]

Cerulo, V. and Cerulo, M. J. (2004). Business continuity planning: A comprehensive approach, *ISM Journal*, Summer, 2017, 21(3), 70–78.

Chatterjee, S., Wiseman, R. M., Fiegenbaum, A. and Devers, C. E. (2003). Integrating behavioural and economic concepts of risk into strategic management: The twain shall meet, *Long Range Planning*, 36(1), 61–79.

Chenhall, R. H. (2003). Management control systems design within its organizational context: Findings from contingency-based research and directions for the future, *Accounting, Organizations and Society*, 28(2–3), 127–168.

Chockalingam, A., Dabadhgao, S. and Soetekouw, R. (2018). Strategic risks, banks, and Basel III: Estimating economic capital requirements, *The Journal of Risk Finance*, 19(3), 225–246.

Christiansen, U. and Thrane, S. (2014). The prose of action: The micro dynamics of reporting on emerging risks in operational risk management, *Scandinavian Journal of Management*, 30, 427–443.

Christopher, M. and Peck, H. (2004). Building the resilient supply chain, *The International Journal of Logistics Management*, 15(2), 1–13.

Cohen, K. J. and Cyert, R. M. (1973). Strategy: Formulation, implementation, and monitoring, *Journal of Business*, 46(3), 349–367.

Collier, P., Berry, A. J. and Burke, G. T. T. (2006). *Risk and Management Accounting: Best Practice Guidelines for Enterprise-wide Internal Control Procedures*. The Chartered Institute of Management Accountants, London, UK.

Corvellec, H. (2009). The practice of risk management: Silence is not absence, *Risk Management*, 11(3–4), 285–304.

COSO. (2004). *Enterprise Risk Management – Integrated Framework*. The Committee of Sponsoring Organizations of the Treadway Commission (COSO). [https://www.coso.org/Documents/COSO-ERM-Executive-Summary.pdf]

COSO. (2014). *How the COSO Frameworks Can Help – Improving Organizational Performance and Governance*. Committee of Sponsoring Organizations of the Treadway Commission (COSO). [https://www.coso.org/Documents/2014-2-10-COSO-Thought-Paper.pdf]

COSO. (2017). *Enterprise Risk Management — Integrating with Strategy and Performance*. The Committee of Sponsoring Organizations of the Treadway Commission (COSO). [https://www.coso.org/Documents/2017-COSO-ERM-Integrating-with-Strategy-and-Performance-Executive-Summary.pdf]

Culp, C. L. (2001). *The Risk Management Process: Business Strategy and Tactics*. Wiley, New York, NY.

Cyert, J. G. and March, R. (1963). *A Behavioral Theory of the Firm* (2nd ed.), Wiley-Blackwell, Hoboken, NJ.

Daft, R. L., Sormunen, J. and Parks, D. (1988). Chief executive scanning, environmental characteristics, and company performance: An empirical study, *Strategic Management Journal*, 9(2), 123–139.

Daft, R. L. and Weick, K. E. (1984). Toward of organizations as model interpretation systems, *The Academy of Management Review*, 9(2), 284–295.

Damodaran, A. (2007). *Strategic Risk Taking: A Framework for Risk Management*. Pearson Prentice Hall, Upper Saddle River, NJ.

Damodaran, A. (2010). Equity Risk Premiums (ERP): Determinants, Estimation and Implications. New York University Stern School of Business [http://people.stern.nyu.edu/adamodar/pdfiles/papers/ERP2010.pdf]

Dean, J. W. and Sharfman, M. P. (1996). Does decision process matter? A study of strategic decisions making effectiveness, *Academy of Management Journal*, 39(2), 368–396.

Delmar, F. and Shane, S. (2003). Does business planning facilitate the development of new ventures? *Strategic Management Journal*, 24(12), 1165–1185.

Desender, K. A. and Lafuente, E. (2011). The relationship between enterprise risk management and external audit fees: Are they complements or substitutes? In Jalilvand, A. and Malliaris, T. (eds.), *Risk Management and Corporate Governance*. Routledge, New York, NY.

Dess, G. G. (1987). Consensus on strategy formulation and organizational performance: Competitors in a fragmented industry, *Strategic Management Journal*, 8(3), 259–277.

Detert, J. R. and Burris, E. R. (2007). Leadership behaviour and employee voice: Is the door really open? *The Academy of Management Journal*, 50(4), 869–884.

Dickinson, G. (2001). Enterprise risk management: Its origins and conceptual foundation. *The Geneva Papers on Risk and Insurance*, 26(3), 360–366.

Doughty K. 2011. The three lines of defense related to risk governance. *ISACA Journal*. [www.isaca.org/Journal/archives/2011/Volume-5/Pages/The-Three-Lines-of-Defence-Related-to-Risk-Governance.aspx]

Drucker, P. F. (1974). *Management: Tasks, Responsibilities and Practices*. Harper & Row, New York, NY.

Dutton, J. E. and Ashford, S. J. (1993). Selling issues to top management, *The Academy of Management Review*, 18(3), 397–428.

Dutton, J. E., Ashford, S. J., O'Neill, R. M., Hayes, E. and Wierba, E. E. (1997). Reading the wind: How middle managers assess the context for selling issues to top managers, *Strategic Management Journal*, 18(5), 407–425.

Dutton, J. E. and Dukerich, J. M. (1991). Keeping an eye on the mirror: Image and identity in organizational adaptation, *Academy of Management Journal*, 34, 517–554.

Dutton, J. E. and Duncan, R. B. (1987a). The creation of momentum for change through the process of strategic issue diagnosis, *Strategic Management Journal*, 8, 279–295.

Dutton, J. E. and Duncan, R. B. (1987b). The influence of the strategic planning process on strategic change, *Strategic Management Journal*, 8, 103–116.

Dutton, J. E., Fahey, J. L. and Narayanan, V. K. (1983). Toward understanding strategic issue diagnosis, *Strategic Management Journal*, 4, 307–323.

Dutton, J. E. and Ottensmeyer, E. (1987). Strategic issue management-systems – Forms, functions, and contexts, *Academy of Management Review*, 12(2), 355–365.

ECIIA. (2013). Our Current Views: Three Lines of Defense. The European Confederation of Institutes of Internal Auditing (ECIIA). [www.eciia.eu/current_views/three-lines-of-defence/]

Eckles, D. L., Hoyt, R. E. and Miller, S. M. (2014a). International diversification and analysts' forecast accuracy and bias, *The Accounting Review*, 77(2), 415–433.

Eckles, D. L., Hoyt, R. E. and Miller, S. M. (2014b). The impact of enterprise risk management on the marginal cost of reducing risk: Evidence from the insurance industry, *Journal of Banking & Finance*, 43, 247–261.

Eisenhardt, K. M. (1989). Making fast strategic decisions in high-velocity environments, *Academy of Management Journal*, 32(3), 543–576.

Eisenhardt, K. M. and Martin, J. A. (2000). Dynamic capabilities: What are they? *Strategic Management Journal*, 21(10–11), 1105–1121.

Fahey, L. and King, W. R. (1977). Environmental scanning for corporate planning, *Business Horizons*, 20(4), 61–71.

Falshaw, J. R., Glaister, K. W. and Tatoglu, E. (2006). Evidence on formal strategic planning and company performance, *Management Decision*, 44(1), 9–30.

FEMA. (2013). *Continuity Plan Template*. Federal Emergency Management Agency (FEMA), Washington, DC.

FERMA/ECIIA. (2011). Guidance on the 8th EU Company Law Directive. Audit and Risk Committees News from EU Legislation and Best Practices. The Federation of Europena Risk Management Associations (FERMA) & The European Confederation of Institutes of Internal Auditing (ECIIA), Brussels, Belgium. [www.ferma.eu/app/uploads/2014/10/ECIIA_FERMA_Brochure_v8.pdf]

FERMA/ECIIA. (2014). Guidance on the 8th EU Company Law Directive – Article 41, Guidance for Boards and Audit Committees, Part 1. The Federation of Europena Risk Management Associations (FERMA) & The European Confederation of Institutes of Internal Auditing (ECIIA), Brussels, Belgium. [www.ferma.eu/app/uploads/2011/09/eciia-ferma-guidance-on-the-8th-eu-company-law-directive.pdf]

Fiegenbaum, A. and Thomas, H. (1986). Dynamic and risk measurement perspectives on Bowman's risk–return paradox for strategic management: An empirical study, *Strategic Management Journal*, 7(5), 395–407.

Fiegenbaum, A. and Thomas, H. (2004). Strategic risk and competitive advantage: An integrative perspective, *European Management Review*, 1(1), 84–95.

Floyd, S. W. and Wooldridge, B. (1997). Middle management's strategic influence and organizational performance, *Journal of Management Studies*, 34(3), 465–485.

Fraser, J. R. S., Schoening-Thiessen, K. and Simkins, B. J. (2008). Who reads what most often? A survey of enterprise risk management literature read by risk executives, *Journal of Applied Finance*, (Spring/Summer), 73–91.

Fraser, J. R. S. and Simkins, B. J. J. (eds.) (2009). *Enterprise Risk Management: Today's Leading Research and Best Practices for Tomorrow's Executives*. Wiley, Hoboken, NJ.

Frigo, M. L. and Anderson, R. J. (2011, April). What is strategic risk management? *Strategic Finance*, 92(10), 21.

Frigo, M. L. and Læssøe, K. (2012, February). Strategic risk management at the LEGO Group, *Strategic Finance*, 93(8), 27.

Froot, K., Scharfstein, D. and Stein, J. (1993). Risk management: Coordinating corporate investment and financing policies, *Journal of Financial Economics*, 48(1), 55–82.

Frow, N., Marginson, D. E. W. and Ogden, S. (2010). "Continuous" budgeting: Reconciling budget flexibility with budgetary control, *Accounting, Organizations and Society*, 35(4), 444–461.

Garg, V. K., Walters, B. A. and Priem, R. L. (2003). Chief executive scanning emphases, environmental dynamism, and manufacturing firm performance. *Strategic Management Journal*, 24(8), 725–744.

Gates, S., Nicolas, J. and Walker, P. L. (2012). Enterprise risk management: A process for enhanced management and improved performance, *Management Accounting Quarterly*, 13(3), 28–38.

Gatzert, N. and Martin, M. (2015) Determinants and value of enterprise risk management: Empirical evidence from the literature, *Risk Management and Insurance Review*, 18(1), 29–53.

Gavetti, G., Levinthal, D. A. and Rivkin, J. W. (2005). Strategy making in novel and complex worlds: The power of analogy, *Strategic Management Journal*, 26(8), 691–712.

Gephart, R. P., Van Maanen, J. and Oberlechner, T. (2009). Organizations and risk in late modernity, *Organization Studies*, 30(2–3), 141–155.

Ghoshal, S. (1987). Global strategy: An organizing framework, *Strategic Management Journal*, 8(5), 425–440.

Golshan, N. M. and Rasid, S. Z. A. (2012). Determinants of enterprise risk management adoption: An empirical analysis of Malaysian public listed firms, *World Academy of Science, Engineering and Technology*, 62(2012), 119–126.

Gooding, R. Z. and Kinicki, A. J. (1995). Interpreting event causes: The complementary role of categorization and attribution processes, *Journal of Management Studies*, 32(1), 1–22.

Goold, M. and Quinn, J. J. (1990). The paradox of strategic controls, *Strategic Management Journal*, 11(1), 43–57.

Gordon, L. A., Loeb, M. P. and Tseng, C. (2009). Enterprise risk management and firm performance: A contingency perspective, *Journal of Accounting and Public Policy*, 28(4), 301–327.

Grace, M. F., Leverty, J. T., Phillips, R. D. and Shimpi, P. (2014). The value of investing in enterprise risk management, *Journal of Risk and Insurance*, 82(2), 289–316.

Grant, R. M. (2003). Strategic planning in a turbulent environment: Evidence from the oil majors, *Strategic Management Journal*, 24, 491–517.

Greenley, G. E. (1994). Strategic planning and company performance: An appraisal of the empirical evidence, *Scandinavian Journal of Management*, 10(4), 383–396.

Gul, F. A. and Chia, Y. M. (1994). The effects of management accounting systems, perceived environmental uncertainty and decentralization on managerial performance: A test of three-way interaction, *Accounting, Organizations and Society*, 19(4–5), 413–426.

Hallegatte, S. and Dumas, P. (2009). Can natural disasters have positive consequences? Investigating the role of embodied technical change, *Ecological Economics*, 68 (3), 777–786.

Hambrick, D. C. (1981). Specialization of environmental scanning activities among upper level executives, *Journal of Management Studies*, 18(3), 299–320.

Hambrick, D. C. (1982). Environmental organizational scanning strategy, *Strategic Management Journal*, 3(2), 159–174.

Hambrick, D. C. (2007). Upper echelons theory: An update, *Academy of Management Review*, 32(2), 334–343.

Hardy, C. and Maguire, S. (2016). Organizing risk: Discourse, power, and "riskification", *Academy of Management Review*, 41(1), 80–108.

Hart, S. L. (1992). An integrative framework for strategy-making processes, *The Academy of Management Review*, 17(2), 327–351.

Henkel, J. (*2009*). The risk-return paradox for strategic management: Disentangling true and spurious effects, *Strategic Management Journal*, 30, 287–303.

Henri, J. (2006). Management control systems and strategy: A resource-based perspective, *Accounting, Organizations and Society*, 31, 529–558.

Henriksen, P. (2018). *Enterprise Risk Management* – Rationaler og paradokser i en moderne ledelsesteknologi. Doctoral School of Business and Management, Copenhagen Business School.

Heugens, P. P. (2001). *Strategic Issues Management: Implications for Corporate Performance*. Erasmus Research Institute of Management, Rotterdam, the Netherlands. [https://core.ac.uk/download/pdf/18510378.pdf]

Hirschborn, L. (1999). The primary risk, *Human Relations*, 52(1), 5–23.

Hitt, M. A. and Tyler, B. B. (1991). Strategic decision models: Integrating different perspectives, *Strategic Management Journal*, 12(5), 327–351.

Hofmann, S., Wald, A. and Gleich, R. (2012). Determinants and effects of the diagnostic and interactive use of control systems: An empirical analysis on the use of budgets, *Journal of Management Control*, 23, 153–182.

Holmen, M. and Pramborg, B. (2009). Capital budgeting and political risk: Empirical evidence, *Journal of International Financial Management and Accounting*, 20(2), 105–134.

Hope, J. and Fraser, R. (2003). *Beyond Budgeting: How Managers Can Break Free From the Annual Performance Trap*. Harvard Business School Press, Boston, MA.

Horngren, C. T., Foster, G. and Datar, S. (1994). *Cost Accounting: A Managerial Emphasis* (8th ed.). Prentice Hall, Englewood Cliffs, NJ.

Hoskisson, R., Chirico, F., Zyung, J. and Gambeta, E. (2017). Managerial risk taking: A multi-theoretical review and future research agenda, *Journal of Management*, 43(1), 137–169.

Hoyt, R. E. and Liebenberg, A. P. (2011). The value of enterprise risk management, *Journal of Risk and Insurance*, 78(8), 795–822.

Husted, B. W. (2005). Risk management, real options, and corporate social responsibility, *Journal of Business Ethics*, 60(2), 175–183.

IIA. (2009). The Role of Internal Auditing in Enterprise-wide Risk Management. Institute of Internal Auditors (IIA). [https://na.theiia.org/Pages/IIA Home.aspx]

IIA. (2013). The Three Lines of Defense in Effective Risk Management and Control, The Institute of Internal Auditors (IIA), Position Paper, Altamonte Springs, FL.

IRM. (2002). *A Risk Management Standard*. The Institute of Risk Management (IRM), London, UK. [www.theirm.org/media/886059/ARMS_2002_ IRM.pdf]

IRM. (2010). *A Structured Approach to Enterprise Risk Management (ERM) and the Requirements of ISO 31000*. The Institute of Risk Management (IRM), London, UK.

IRM. (2018). *A Risk Practioners Guide to ISO 31000: 2018*. Institute of Risk Management (IRM), London, UK.

ISO. (2009). ISO 31000: 2009 Risk Management – Principles and Guidelines. The International Organization for Standardization (ISO), Geneva, Switzerland.

ISO. (2018). ISO 31000: 2018 Risk Management – Guidelines. The International Organization for Standardization (ISO), Geneva, Switzerland.

ISO/IEC. (2002). *Guide 73, Risk Management – Vocabulary – Guidelines for Use in Standards*. International Organization for Standardization (ISO)/ International Electrotechnical Commission (IEC), Geneva, Switzerland.

Ittner, C. D. and Keusch, T. (2016). Incorporating risk considerations into planning and control systems: The influence of risk management value creation objectives, In Woods, M. and Lindsey, P. (eds.), *The Routledge Companion to Accounting and Risk*, Routledge, Abingdon, UK, 150–171.

Jensen, M. C. and Meckling, W. H. (1976). Theory of the firm: Managerial behavior, agency costs and ownership structure, *Journal of Financial Economics*, 3(4), 305–360.

Johnson, G., Langley, A., Melin, L. and Whittington, R. (2007). *Strategy as Practice. Research Directions and Resources*. Cambridge University Press, Cambridge, UK.

Johnson, G., Scholes, K. and Whittington, R. (2006). *Exploring Corporate Strategy*. FT-Prentice Hall, London, UK.

Jordan, A., Jørgensen, L. and Mitterhofer, H. (2013). Performing risk and the project: Risk maps as mediating instruments, *Management Accounting Research*, 24(2), 156–174. [doi:10.1016/j.mar.2013.04.009]

Kahneman, D. and Tversky, A. (1979). Prospect theory: An analysis of decision under risk, *Econometrica*, 47(2), 263–292.

Kanter, R. M. (1982). The middle manager as innovator, *Harvard Business Review*, 82(7/8), 150–161.

Keown, A. J., Martin, J. D. and Petty, J. (2008). *Foundation of Finance: The Logic and Practice of Financial Management*. Prentice Hall, London, UK.

Ketokivi, M. and Castañer, X. (2004). Strategic planning as an integrative device, *Administrative Science Quarterly*, 49(3), 337–365.

Kiesler, S. and Sproull, L. (1982). Managerial response to changing environments: Perspectives on problem sensing from social cognition, *Administrative Science Quarterly*, 27(4), 548–70.

King, A. W. and Zeithaml, C. P. (2001). Competencies and firm performance: Examining the causal ambiguity paradox, *Strategic Management Journal*, 22(1), 75–99.

King, W. (1982). Using strategic issue analysis in long range planning, *Long Range Planning*, 15, 45–49.

Kleffner, E., Lee, R. B. and McGannon, B. (2003). The effect of corporate governance on the use of enterprise risk management: Evidence from Canada, *Risk Management and Insurance Review*, 6(1), 53–73.

Kloot, L. (1997). Organizational learning and management control systems: Responding to environmental change, *Management Accounting Research*, 8, 47–73.

Knight, F. H. (1921). *Risk, Uncertainty, and Profit*. Houghton Mifflin, Boston, MA.

Knight, R. F. and Pretty, D. J. (2005). Protecting Value in the Face of Mass Fatality Events. *Oxford Metrica*. [http://oxfordmetrica.com/public/CMS/Files/601/04RepComKen.pdf]

Knights, D. and Morgan, G. (1991). Corporate strategy, organizations, and subjectivity: A critique, *Organization Studies*, 12(2), 251–273.

Kober, R., Ng, J. and Paul, B. J. (2007). The interrelationship between management control mechanisms and strategy, *Management Accounting Research*, 18, 425–452.

KPMG. (2011). *Risk Management: A Driver of Enterprise Value in the Emerging Environment*, KPMG Survey. KPMG International, Zug, Switzerland.

Kraus, V. and Lehner, O. M. (2012). The nexus of enterprise risk management and value creation: A systematic literature review, *ACRN Journal of Finance and Risk Perspective*, 1(1), 91–163.

Krause, T. A. and Tse, Y. (2016). Risk management and firm value: Recent theory and evidence, *International Journal of Accounting and Information Management*, 24(1), 56–81.

Kroszner, R. S. (2008). Strategic risk management in an interconnected world. *BIS Review* 127/2008, 1–7. Speech at the Risk Management Association Annual Risk Management Conference.

Lam, J. C. (2003) *Enterprise Risk Management: From Incentives to Controls*. Wiley, Hoboken, NJ.

Lam, J. C. (2014). *Risk Management: From Incentives to Controls*. Wiley, Hoboken, NJ.

Lam, J. C. and Kawamoto, B. M. (1997). Emergence of the chief risk officer, *Risk Management*, 44(9), 30–36.

Langley, A. (1990). Patterns in the use of formal analysis in strategic decision, *Organization Studies*, 11(1), 17–45.

Lant, T. K., Milliken, F. J. and Batra, B. (1992). The role of managerial learning and interpretation in strategic persistence and reorientation: An empirical exploration, *Strategic Management Journal*, 13(8), 585–608.

Leland, H. E. and Pyle, D. H. (1977). Informational asymmetries, financial structure, and financial intermediation, *The Journal of Finance*, 32(2), 371–387.

Liebenberg, A. P. and Hoyt, R. E. (2003). The determinants of enterprise risk management: Evidence from the appointment of Chief Risk Officers, *Risk Management and Insurance Review*, 6(1), 37–52.

Liedtka, J. (2000). Strategic planning as a contributor to strategic change: A generative model, *European Management Journal*, 18(2), 195–206.

Lin, Y., Wen, M. and Yu, J. (2012). Enterprise risk management: Strategic antecedents, risk integration, and performance, *North American Actuarial Journal*, 16(1), 1–28.

Lippman, S. A. and Rumelt, R. P. (1982). Uncertain imitability: An analysis of interfirm differences in efficiency under competition, *Bell Journal of Economics*, 13(2), 418–438.

Lorange, P. (1977). Strategic control: A framework for effective response to environmental change. Working Paper, MIT Sloan School of Management.

Lundquist, S. A. (2014). An exploratory study of enterprise risk management: Pillars of ERM, *Journal of Accounting, Auditing & Finance*, 29(3), 393–429.

Lundqvist, S. A. and Vilhelmsson, A. (2018). Enterprise risk management and default risk: Evidence from the banking industry, *The Journal of Risk and Insurance*, 85(1), 127–157.

Lyons, S. (2011). Corporate Oversight and Stakeholder Lines of Defense. Action Report, No. 365, The Conference Board. [https://papers.ssrn.com/sol3/papers.cfm?abstract_id=1938360]

Mahnke, V., Venzin, M. and Zahra, S. A. (2007). Governing entrepreneurial opportunity recognition in MNEs: Aligning interests and cognition under uncertainty, *Journal of Management Studies*, 44(7), 1278–1298.

Manuj, I. and Mentzer, J. T. (2008). Global supply chain risk management strategies, *International Journal of Physical Distribution & Logistics Management*, 38(3), 192–223.

March, J. G. and Shapira, Z. (1987). Managerial perspectives on risk and risk taking, *Management Science*, 33(11), 1404–1418.

Marginson, D. E. W. (2002). Management control systems and their effects on strategy formation at middle-management levels: Evidence from a U.K. organization, *Strategic Management Journal*, 23, 1019–1031.

Martin, D. and Power, M. (2007). *The End of Enterprise Risk Management*, AEI-Brookings Joint Center for Regulatory Studies, Washington, DC.

Mascarenhas, B. (1982). Uncertainty in international business. *Journal of International Business Studies*, 13(2), 87–98.

McShane, M. (2018). Enterprise risk management: History and a design science proposal, *The Journal of Risk Finance*, 19(2), 137–153.

McShane, M. K., Nair, A. and Rustambekov, E. (2011). Does enterprise risk management increase firm value? *Journal of Accounting, Auditing & Finance*, 26(4), 641–658.

Merton, R. C. (2005). You have more capital than you think, *Harvard Business Review*, 83(11), 84–94.

Meulbroek, L. K. (2002). A senior manager's guide to integrated risk management, *Journal of Applied Corporate Finance*, 14(4), 56–70.

Meyer, A. D. (1982). Adapting to environmental jolts, *Administrative Science Quarterly*, 27(4), 515–537.

Miccolis, J. and Shah, S. (2000). *Enterprise Risk Management: An Analytic Approach.* Tillinghast-Towers Perrin, New York, NY.

Mikes, A. (2005). Enterprise Risk Management in Action. ESRC Centre for Analysis of Risk and Regulation Discussion Paper.

Mikes, A. (2009). Risk management and calculative cultures, *Management Accounting Research*, 20(1), 18–40.

Mikes, A. (2014). The Triumph of the Humble Chief Risk Officer, Harvard Business School, Working Paper.

Mikes, A. and Kaplan, R. (2014). Towards a contingency theory of enterprise risk management. *Harvard Business School*, Working Paper. [www.hbs.edu/faculty/Publication%20Files/13-063_5e67dffe-aa5e-4fac-a746-7b3c07902520.pdf]

Miller, C. C., Burke, L. M. and Glick, W. H. (1998). Cognitive diversity among upper echelon executives: Implications for strategic decision processes, *Strategic Management Journal*, 19, 29–58.

Miller, C. C. and Cardinal, L. B. (1994). Strategic planning and firm performance: A synthesis of more than two decades of research, *Academy of Management Journal*, 37(6), 1649–1665.

Miller, D. and Friesen, P. H. (1978). Strategy-making in context: Ten empirical archetypes, *Journal of Management Studies*, 14(3), 253–280.

Miller, K. D. (1992). A framework for integrated risk management in international business, *Journal of International Business Studies*, 23(2), 311–331.

Miller, K. D. and Bromiley, P. (1990). Strategic risk and corporate performance: An analysis of alternative risk measures, *The Academy of Management Journal*, 33(4), 756–779.

Miller, K. D. and Leiblein, M. J. (1996). Corporate risk-return relations: Returns variability versus downside risk, *Academy of Management Journal*, 39(1), 91–122.

Milliken, F. J. (1990). Perceiving and interpreting environmental change: An examination of college administrators' interpretation of changing demographics, *The Academy of Management Journal*, 33(1), 42–63.

Mintzberg, H. (1978). Patterns in strategy formation, *Management Science*, 24(9), 934–948.

Mintzberg, H., Ahlstrand, B. and Lampel, J. (1998). *Strategy Safari: A Guided Tour Through the Wilds of Strategic.* The Free Press, New York, NY.

Mintzberg, H., Raisinghani, D. and Théorêt, A. (1976). The structure of "un-structured" decision processes, *Administrative Science Quarterly*, 21(2), 246–275.

Mintzberg, H. and Waters, J. A. (1982). Tracking strategy in an entrepreneurial firm, *Academy of Management Journal*, 25(3), 465–499.

Mintzberg, H. and Waters, J. A. (1985). Of strategies, deliberate and emergent, *Strategic Management Journal*, 6(3), 257–272.

Moeller, R. (2007). *COSO Enterprise Risk Management: Understanding the New Integrated ERM Framework*. Wiley, Hoboken, NJ.

Moffett, M. H., Stonehill, A. I. and Eiteman, D. K. (2008). *Fundamentals of Multinational Finance*. Addison-Wesley, Boston, MA. (First edition 1988).

Mueller, G. C., Mone, M. A. and Barker, V. L. (2007). Formal strategic analyses and organizational performance: Decomposing the rational model, *Organization Studies*, 29(6), 853–883.

Myers, S. C. (1977). Determinants of corporate borrowing, *Journal of Financial Economics*, 5, 147–175.

Nair, A., Rustambekov, E., Mcshane, M. and Fainshmidt, S. (2014). Enterprise risk management as a dynamic capability: A test of its effectiveness during a crisis, *Managerial and Decision Economics*, 35(8), 555–566.

Naranjo-Gil, D. and Hartmann, F. (2007). Management accounting systems, top management team heterogeneity and strategic change, *Accounting, Organizations and Society*, 32(7–8), 735–756.

Nickel, M. N. and Rodriguez, M. C. (2002). A review of research on the negative accounting relationship between risk and return: Bowman's paradox, *Omega*, 30, 1–18.

Nielson, N. L., Kleffner, A. E., and Lee, R. B. (2005). The evolution of the role of risk communication in effective risk management, *Risk Management & Insurance Review*, 8(2), 279–289.

Nocco, B. W. amd Stulz, R. M. (2006). Enterprise risk management: Theory and practice, *Journal of Applied Corporate Finance*, 18, 8–20.

O'Brien, J. P. (2003). The capital structure implications of pursuing a strategy of innovation, *Strategic Management Journal*, 24(5), 415–431.

Ocasio, W. (1997). Towards an attention-based view of the firm, *Strategic Management Journal*, 18, 187–206.

OECD. (2014). *Risk Management and Corporate Governance*, Corporate Governance. OECD Publishing. [http.//dx.doi.org/10.1787/9789264208636-en]

Oetzel, J. and Miklian, J. (2017). Multinational enterprises, risk management, and the business and economics of peace, *Multinational Business Review*, 25(4), 270–286.

Ohmae, K. (1982). *The Mind of the Strategist: Business Planning for Competitive Advantage*. Penguin, Lodon, UK.

O'Regan, N., Sims, M. A. and Gallear, D. (2008). Leaders, loungers, laggards: The strategic-planning-environment-performance relationship re-visited in manufacturing SMEs, *Journal of Manufacturing Technology Management*, 19(1), 6–21.

Otley, D. T. (1999). Performance management: A framework for management control systems research, *Management Accounting Research*, 10(4), 363–382.

Paape, L. and Speklé, R. F. (2012). The adoption and design of enterprise risk management practices: An empirical study, *European Accounting Review*, 21(3), 533–564.

Pablo, A. L., Sitkin, S. and Jemison, D. B. (1996). Acquisition decision-making process: The central role of risk, *Journal of Management*, 22(5), 723–746.

Pagach, D. and Warr, R. (2011). The characteristics of firms that hire Chief Risk Officers, *Journal of Risk and Insurance*, 78(1), 185–211.

Paine, F. T. and Anderson, C. R. (1977). Contingencies affecting strategy formulation and effectiveness: An empirical study, *Journal of Management Studies*, 14, 147–158.

Pascale, R. T. (1984). Perspectives on strategy: The real story behind Honda's success, *California Management Review*, 26(3), 47–72.

Pernell, K., Jung, J. and Dobbin, F. (2017). The hazards of expert control: Chief risk officers and risky derivatives, *American Sociological Review*, 82(3), 511–541.

Peteraf, M. A., Di Stefano, G. and Verona, G. (2013). The elephant in the room of dynamic capabilities: Bringing two diverging conversations together, *Strategic Management Journal*, 34(12), 1389–1410.

Pierce, E. M. and Goldstein, J. (2018). ERM and strategic planning: A change in paradigm, *International Journal of Disclosure and Governance*, 15, 51–59.

Porter, M. E. (1979). How competitive forces shape strategy, *Harvard Business Review*, 57(2), 137–145.

Porter, M. E. (1996) What is strategy? *Harvard Business Review*, 73(6), 61–78.

Power, M. (2003). Evaluating the audit explosion, *Law & Policy*, 25(3), 185–202.

Power, M. (2004). The risk management of everything, *The Journal of Risk Finance*, 5(3), 58–65.

Power, M. (2007). *Organized Uncertainty: Designing a World of Risk Management*. Oxford University Press, Oxford, UK.

Power, M. (2009). The risk management of nothing, *Accounting, Organization and Society*, 34(6–7), 849–855.

Preble, J. F. (1992). Towards a comprehensive system of strategic control, *Journal of Management Studies*, 29(4), 391–409.

Priem, R. L., Rasheed, A. M. A. and Kotulic, A. G. (1995). Rationality in strategic decision processes, environmental dynamism and firm performance, *Journal of Management*, 21(5), 913–929.

Quinn, J. J. (1996). The role of "good conversation" in strategic control, *Journal of Management Studies*, 33(3), 381–394.

Quon, T. K., Zeghal, D. and Maingot, M. (2012). Enterprise risk management and firm performance, *Procedia – Social and Behavioral Sciences*, 62, 263–267.

Reed, R. and Defillippi, R. J. (1990). Causal ambiguity, barriers to imitation, and sustainable competitive advantage, *Academy of Management Review*, 15(1), 88–102.

Reuer, J. J. and Leiblein, M. J. (2000). Downside risk implications of multinationality and international joint ventures, *Academy of Management Journal*, 43(2), 203–214.

Rienkhemaniyom, K. and Ravindran, A. R. (2014). Global supply chain network design incorporating disruption risk, *International Journal of Business Analytics*, 1(3), 39–64.

RIMS. (2011). Risk and Insurance Management Society. Why Strategic Risk Management? Risk Management and Insurance Society (RIMS) White Paper. [www.rims.org/resources/ERM/Documents/FAQ%20on%20 SRM%20and%20ERM%20FINAL%20April%2020%202011.pdf]

RIMS. (2017). Enterprise Risk Management: Benchmark Survey. Risk Management and Insurance Society (RIMS). [www.rims.org/RiskKnowledge/ RISKKnowledgeDocs/2017_ERM_survey_1162017_84825.pdf]

Roberts, J. (1990). Strategy and accounting in a U.K. conglomerate, *Accounting, Organizations and Society*, 15(1–2), 107–126.

Rochette, M. (2009). From risk management to ERM, *Journal of Risk Management in Financial Institutions*, 2(4), 394–408.

Ruefli, T. (1990). Mean-variance approaches to risk-return relationships in strategy: Paradox lost, *Management Science*, 36(3), 368–380.

Ruefli, T. W., Collins, J. M., Lacugna, J. R. and Wiley, J. (1999). Risk measures in strategic management research: auld lang syne? *Strategic Management Journal*, 20(2), 167–194.

Samuelson, W. and Zeckhauser, R. (1988). Status quo bias in decision-making, *Journal of Risk and Uncertainty*, 1, 7–59.

Sax, J. and Andersen, T. J. (2018). Making risk management strategic: Integrating enterprise risk management with strategic planning. *European Management Review*. [doi:10.1111/emre.12185]

Sax, J. and Torp, S. (2015). Speak up! Enhancing risk performance with enterprise risk management, leadership style and employee voice, *Management Decision*, 53(7), 1452–1468.

Schendel, D. and Hofer, C. (1979). *Strategic Management: A New View of Business Policy and Planning*. Little, Brown, Boston, MA.

Scheytt, T., Soin, K., Sahlin-Andersson, K. and Power, M. (2006). Organizations, risk and regulation, *Journal of Management Studies*, 43(6), 1331–1337.

Schiller, F. and Prpich, G. (2014). Learning to organise risk management in organisations: What future for enterprise risk management? *Journal of Risk Research*, 17(8), 999–1017. doi:10.1080/13669877.2013.841725

Schreyogg, G. and Steinmann, H. (1987). Strategic control: A new perspective, *Academy of Management Review*, 12(1), 91–103.

Schulman, P., Roe, E., van Eeten, M. and de Bruijne, M. (2016). High reliability and the management of critical infrastructures. In Andersen, T. J. (ed.), *The Routledge Companion to Strategic Risk Management*, Routledge, Abingdon, UK, 463–481.

Scott, W. G., Mitchell, T. R. and Birnbaum, P. H. (1981). *Organization Theory: A Structural and Behavioral Analysis*. Irwin, Homewood, IL.

Senge, P. M. (1990). *The Fifth Discipline: The At and Practice of the Learning Organization*. Doubleday, New York, NY.

Seville, E., Stevenson, J. R., Vargo, J., Brown, C. and S. Giovinazzi, S. (2015). Resilience and recovery: Business behavior following the Canterbury earthquakes. In Ayyub, B. M., Chapman, R. E., Galloway, G. E. and Wright, R. N. (eds.), *Economics of Community Disaster Resilience Workshop Proceedings*. NIST Special Publication 1600, National Institute of Standards and Technology (NIST), Gaithersburg, MD, 177–183.

Shapira, Z. (1995). *Risk Taking: A Managerial Perspective*. Sage, New York, NY.

Sheehan, G. A. (1975). *Long-Range Strategic Planning and Its Relationship to Firm Size, Firm Growth, and Firm Growth Variability.* University of Western Ontario, London, ON.

Shimizu, K. and Hitt, M. A. (2004). Strategic flexibility: Organizational preparedness to reverse ineffective strategic decisions, *The Academy of Management Execut ive*, 18(4), 44–59.

Shoemaker, P. J. H. and Day, G. S. (2009). How to make sense of weak signals, *MIT-Sloan Management Review*, 50(3), 81–89.

Shrader, B. C., Taylor, L. and Dalton, D. R. (1984). Strategic planning and organizational performance: A critical appraisal, *Journal of Management*, 10(2), 149–171.

Simons, R. (1987). Accounting control systems and business strategy: An empirical analysis, *Accounting, Organizations and Society*, 12(4), 357–374.

Simons, R. (1991). Strategic orientiation and top management attention to control systems, *Strategic Management Journal*, 12, 49–62.

Simons, R. (1994). How new top managers use control systems as levers of strategic renewal, *Strategic Management Journal*, 15(3), 169–189.

Simons, R. (1995a). Control in an age of empowerment. *Harvard Business Review*, 73(2), 80–88.

Simons, R. (1995b). *Levers of Control: How Managers Use Innovative Control Systems to Drive Strategic Renewal.* Harvard Business School Press, Boston, MA.

Simons, R. (2000). *Performance Measurement and Control Systems for Implementing Strategies.* Prentice Hall, Upper Saddle River, NJ.

Sitkin, S. B. and Pablo, A. L. (1992). Reconceptualizing the determinants of risk behavior, *The Academy of Management Review*, 17(1), 9–38.

Slywotzky, A. J. and Drzik, J. (2005). Countering the biggest risk of all, *Harvard Business Review*, 83(4), 78–88.

Soltanizadeh, S., Rasid, S. Z. A., Golshan N. M. and Ismail, W. K. W. (2016). Business strategy, enterprise risk management and organizational performance, *Management Research Review*, 39(9), 1016–1033.

Spedding, L. S. and Rose, A. (2008). *Business Risk Management Handbook: A Sustainable Approach.* Elsevier, Burlington, MA.

Spee, A. P. and Jarzabkowski, P. (2011). Strategic planning as a communicative process, *Organization Studies*, 26, 1573–1601.

Srivastav, A. and Hagendorff, J. (2016). Corporate governance and bank risk-taking, *Corporate Governance: An International Review*, 24(3), 334–345.

Staw, B. M., Sandelands, L. E. and Dutton, J. E. (1981). Threat rigidity effects in organizational behavior: A multilevel analysis, *Administrative Science Quarterly*, 26(4), 501–524.

Stulz, R. M. (1996). Rethinking risk management, *Journal of Applied Corporate Finance*, 9(3), 8–24.

S&P. (2008). Enterprise Risk Management: Standard & Poor's To Apply Enterprise Risk Analysis To Corporate Ratings, Standard and Poor's Rating Services (S&P). [www.standardandpoors.com/ratingsdirect]

S&P. (2012). Methodology: Management and Governance Credit Factors for Corporate Entities and Insurers. Standard and Poor's Rating Services (S&P). [www.spratings.com/scenario-builder portlet/pdfs/ICSB_Methodology_Corporate_Entities_Insurers.pdf]

Taleb, N. N. (2007a). Black swans and the domains of statistics, *The American Statistician*, 61(3), 1–3.

Taleb, N. N. (2007b). *The Black Swan: The Impact of the Highly Improbable.* Random House, London, UK.

Taleb, N. N. (2009). Errors, robustness, and the fourth quadrant, *International Journal of Forecasting*, 25, 744–759.

Taylor, L. (2014). *Practical Enterprise Risk Management: How to Optimize Business Strategies.* Kogan Page, London, UK.

Teece, D. J. (2007). Explicating dynamic capabilities: The nature and micro-foundations of (sustainable) enterprise performance, *Strategic Management Journal*, 28(13), 1319–1350.

Teece, D. J., Pisano, G. and Shuen, A. (1997). Dynamic capabilities and strategic management, *Strategic Management Journal*, 18(7), 509–533.

The RiskMinds. (2009). Risk Managers Survey: The Causes and Implications of the 2008 Banking Crisis. Moore, Carter & Associates and Cranfield University, March 2010. [www.moorecarter.co.uk/RiskMinds%202009%20Risk%20Managers'%20Survey%20Report.19March2010.pdf]

Thomas, J. B., Clark, S. M. and Gioia, D. A. (1993). Strategic sensemaking and organizational performance: Linkages among scanning, interpretation, action, and outcomes, *The Academy of Management Journal*, 36(2), 239–270.

Thomas, J. B. and McDaniel, R. R. (1990). Interpreting strategic issues: Effects of strategy and the information-processing structure of top management teams, *The Academy of Management Journal*, 33(2), 286–306.

TNDJ. (2012). The Official Report of the Fukushima Nuclear Accident Independent Investigation Commission, The National Diet of Japan (TNDJ). [www.nirs.org/wp-content/uploads/fukushima/naiic_report.pdf]

Tuomela, T. (2005). The interplay of different levers of control: A case study of introducing a new performance measurement system, *Management Accounting Research*, 16, 293–320.

Tversky, A. and Kahneman, D. (1981). The framing of decisions and the psychology of choice, *Science*, 211, 453–458.

Vlek, C. A. J. and Stallen, P. J. (1980). Rational and personal aspects of risk, *Acta Psychologia*, 45, 273–300.

Volberda, H. W. (1996). Toward the flexible form: How to remain vital in hypercompetitive environments, *Organization Science*, 7(4), 359–374.

Voss, G. B., Sirdeshmukh, D. and Voss, Z. G. (2008). The effects of slack resources and environmental threat on product exploration and exploitation, *Academy of Management Journal*, 51(1), 147–164.

Wang, H., Barney, J. B. and Reuer, J. J. (2003). Stimulating firm-specific investment through risk management, *Long Range Planning*, 36(1), 49–58.

Weick, K. E. and Sutcliffe, K. M. (2001). *Managing the Unexpected*, Jossey-Bass, San Francisco, CA.

Weitzel, W. and Jonsson, E. (1989). Decline in organizations: A literature integration and extension, *Administrative Science Quarterly*, 34(1), 91–109.

Weitzner, D. and Darroch, J. (2009). The limits of strategic rationality: Ethics, enterprise risk management, and governance, *Journal of Business Ethics*, 92, 361–372.

Wheelen, T. L. and Hunger, J. D. (2010). *Essentials of Strategic Management* (5th ed.). Prentice Hall, Hoboken, NJ.

Whittington, R. (2006). Completing the practice turn in strategy research, *Organization Studies*, 27(5), 613–634.

Widener, S. K. (2007). An empirical analysis of the levers of control framework, *Accounting, Organizations and Society*, 32, 757–788.

Wiseman, R. M. and Bromiley, P. (1996).Toward a model of risk in declining organizations: An empirical examination of risk, performance and decline, *Organization Science*, 7(5), 469–592.

Wolf, C. and Floyd, S. W. (2013). Strategic planning research: Toward a theory-driven agenda, *Journal of Management*, 43(6), 1754–1788.

Wooldridge, B. and Floyd, S. W. (1990). The strategy process, middle management involvement, and organizational performance, *Strategic Management Journal*, 11(3), 231–241.

Index

Note: **Bold** page numbers refer to tables; *italic* page numbers refer to figures and page numbers followed by "n" denote endnotes.